CITRUS

By the Editors of Sunset Books

SUNSET PUBLISHING CORPORATION ■ MENLO PARK, CALIFORNIA

SUPERB CITRUS

No wonder so many home gardeners enjoy growing citrus! Without demanding too much attention, the myriad citrus varieties produce evergreen foliage, fragrant flowers, and plentiful harvests of colorful fruit. Home growers in mild-winter climates have the most choices, from the familiar lemons and sweet oranges to the more exotic pummelos and limequats. But gardeners elsewhere needn't be left in the cold: they can select hardy varieties or grow citrus in pots that can be sheltered through the winter.

For reviewing the manuscript, we extend sincere thanks to a trio of citrus experts who share an enormous enthusiasm for these plants: John E. Fucik, Texas A&M–Kingsville; David J. Gumpf, University of California, Riverside; and Larry K. Jackson, Florida Department of Agriculture.

Thanks also to William Castle, Mike Kesinger, Joe Knapp, and Robert Rouse in Florida; Mani Skaria in Texas; Glenn Wright and John Loghry in Arizona; Joe Morse, Paul Baca, Bob Zuckerman, Don Dillon Sr., and George Vashel in California; and Jerry Black in Oregon.

Lemon trees yield tangy fruit and screen the yard from a busy street.

First printing February 1996
Copyright © 1996 Sunset Publishing Corporation, Menlo Park, CA 94025. First edition. All rights reserved, including the right of reproduction in whole or in any form.

ISBN 0-376-03104-2
Library of Congress Catalog Card: 95-72514
Printed in the United States.

If you would like to order additional copies of any of our books, call us at 1-800-634-3095 or check with your local bookstore. For special sales, bulk orders, and premium sales information, call Sunset Custom Publishing & Special Sales at (415) 324-5547.

President & Publisher
Susan J. Maruyama

Director, Sales & Marketing
Richard A. Smeby

Director, New Business
Kenneth Winchester

Editorial Director
Bob Doyle

Marketing & Creative Services Manager
Guy C. Joy

Production Director
Lory Day

EDITORIAL STAFF FOR CITRUS

Research & Text
Susan Lang

Coordinating Editor
Suzanne Normand Eyre

Design
Joe di Chiarro

Illustrations
Mimi Osborne
Wendy Smith-Griswold

Copy Editor
Rebecca LaBrum

Production Coordinator
Patricia S. Williams

SUNSET PUBLISHING CORPORATION

Chairman
Jim Nelson

President & Chief Executive Officer
Stephen J. Seabolt

Chief Financial Officer
James E. Mitchell

Publisher, Sunset Magazine
Anthony P. Glaves

Director of Finance
Larry Diamond

Circulation Director
Robert I. Gursha

Vice President, Manufacturing
Lorinda B. Reichert

Editor, Sunset Magazine
William R. Marken

CONTENTS

IRRESISTIBLE CITRUS

Oranges and grapefruit mean sunshine and health! In the early days of the citrus industry, that was the message marketers wanted to send the public. Colorful labels on the fruit crates extolled the virtues of citrus and of the citrus-growing states, luring countless northerners south and west to enjoy the good life amid lush orange groves.

Today, newcomers to the citrus belt still delight in cultivating such exotic fruit. But cold-climate gardeners, too, are drawn to citrus—so much so that they're willing to lug heavy pots indoors and out with the changing seasons, all for the pleasure of producing a few lemons or limes. And even if a tree doesn't bear fruit, its glossy evergreen foliage and fragrant blooms enchant the gardener.

These dedicated citrus lovers are following in the footsteps of northern European monarchs who, beginning in the 15th century, erected glass buildings (later called orangeries) to shelter their cherished citrus trees during cold weather. Despite their riches, though, these sovereigns enjoyed far fewer citrus choices than today's home growers do. Besides the familiar sweet oranges, grapefruits, lemons, and limes, you can try your hand at raising mandarins, calamondins, tangors, tangelos, pummelos, blood oranges, sour oranges, citrons, kumquats, limequats, and orangequats. If you live in a cold-winter region, your options for citrus grown in the ground include such hardy types as nansho daidai, Ichang papeda, and citrange.

Citrus varieties abound. You don't grow just a plain grapefruit tree, but a certain type, such as 'Flame', 'Marsh', 'Rio Red', or 'Redblush'. If you want to cultivate mandarins, you can choose from a long list of selections, among them 'Clementine', 'Dancy', 'Kara', 'Kinnow', 'Ponkan', and several types of satsumas—to name only a few.

The many kinds of citrus cultivated today probably all have their origins in just two or three ancestors that developed thousands of years ago in Southeast Asia. Modern scientists labor hard to produce new varieties with superior flavor and disease resistance, as well

as sorts that ripen at different times of year. Such intensive research and development is motivated by the importance of citrus among commercial fruit crops: worldwide, more citrus is produced than apples, peaches, pears, and all other deciduous tree fruits combined. Of course, home growers needn't concern themselves with big business—for legions of gardeners, the sheer fun and satisfaction are reasons enough to cultivate citrus.

Top: The lemon tree in this home garden contributes good looks in addition to tangy fruit.

Above: Today as they did centuries ago, potted citrus trees summer outdoors at the orangerie at Versailles.

Left: Orange trees thrive in the favorable climate of this commercial grove in Pauma Valley, near San Diego, California.

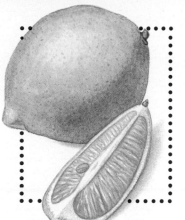

WHERE CITRUS GROWS

Which types of citrus will grow successfully in your garden? The answer to that question is decided by your climate—in particular, by the levels of summer heat and winter cold. Climate also determines whether your trees can be planted in the ground or must be raised in pots and brought indoors for winter. Home citrus-growers living in Florida, California, and other mild-winter regions generally enjoy a greater selection and better results—but gardeners in colder climates can get in on the fun, too.

Hardy 'Changsha' flourishes in areas too cold for conventional mandarin varieties.

FAVORABLE CLIMATES FOR CITRUS

The conventional citrus varieties—oranges, grapefruit, lemons, limes, and so on—thrive outdoors year-round in many tropical and subtropical climates of the world. In the United States, they flourish in the southern-most regions, where summers are warm and winters mild (see "The Citrus Belt," page 11).

The most cold-tolerant types, such as sat-suma mandarins and kumquats, succeed in those borderline climates (see page 10) where winter temperatures often dip below freezing (32°F/0°C) but don't fall much lower than 24°F/-4°C. For colder parts of the borderline region, hardy citrus is available, including such oddities as 'Yuzu' ichandarin and nansho daidai (see pages 88–89). Of course, you can choose conventional citrus in these and even frostier areas if you grow the trees in contain-ers and shelter them in winter.

Whatever variety you choose, the keys to success are the same: you must meet the tree's heat requirement, and you must not exceed its cold tolerance.

Heat Requirement

Citrus varieties differ in the amount of heat they need. As a general rule, fruit that is sup-posed to be sweet requires moderate to high heat to form sugars. Sour-fruited varieties, with the notable exception of 'Mexican' lime, can do with less heat.

Grapefruit demands more heat than any other citrus. Prolonged warmth is crucial both for the fruit's characteristic sweet-tart flavor and, in the case of pigmented varieties, for its red color. In areas of California too cool for good grapefruit, home gardeners can grow the grapefruit-pummelo hybrids 'Melogold' and 'Oroblanco', which need less heat to sweeten.

Top: 'Valencia' orange thrives outdoors in citrus-belt regions with warm summers and mild winters.

Above: Given enough summer heat, 'Redblush' grapefruit succeeds beyond the citrus belt as long as it's raised in a pot and moved to protection in cold weather.

Opposite page: Most commonly used as a root-stock for other citrus varieties, the extremely cold-hardy trifoliate orange is grown as an ornamental in this Virginia garden.

Sweet oranges and mandarins require moderate heat, though most can tolerate high temperatures. Lemons and other sour-fruited citrus will also take considerable heat, but they thrive where summers are mild or even cool. Kumquats, however—despite their tart flesh—need warmth to produce sweet edible rind.

Intense heat is detrimental to some citrus, such as satsuma mandarins, which are not recommended for desert growing.

Cold Tolerance

Among conventional citrus, some types have almost no tolerance for freezing weather, while others can withstand temperatures in the high teens. Lemons, limes, and citrons are the most tender. Sweet oranges, grapefruit, and most mandarins and their hybrids are intermediate; kumquats, satsuma mandarins, sour oranges, and calamondin are the most cold-resistant. Several kinds of hardy citrus endure temperatures near or below zero.

Note that the cold tolerance just outlined applies to the actual trees, not their fruit. Most citrus fruit is damaged at several degrees below freezing, though large types such as pummelos resist a little more cold than do small ones like kumquats. Since citrus ripens only on the tree, you can't salvage a crop by harvesting before maturity.

Exact hardiness figures for citrus aren't very meaningful, since a mature tree's tolerance for cold is determined by many factors, including the health of the tree, the cold tolerance of the rootstock, and location in the garden (see "Taking Advantage of Microclimates," page 17).

A tree's ability to withstand a freeze also depends on whether it has been conditioned to cold that season. Citrus acquires cold resistance by experiencing gradually decreasing temperatures during its near-dormant period. Where frigid weather arrives abruptly and often early, as it does in Texas, a satsuma mandarin is no hardier than a grapefruit. But the same mandarin tree will survive lower temperatures if it is exposed to cold slowly and encounters the first freeze in February rather than December.

As just noted, this sort of cold conditioning helps increase hardiness in citrus that stops growing in winter. Everbearing types such as lemons, limes, and citrons, which produce new growth all year, fall into a different category: they're more vulnerable to cold no matter how or when it comes. Their cold tolerance is greater in very hot-summer areas, where they may produce just one annual crop.

How long the thermometer stays below freezing can be more critical than the actual low temperature. For example, the most sensi-

CITRUS CLIMATES

CITRUS BELT
Conventional citrus varieties can be planted in the ground.

BORDERLINE REGION
The most cold-tolerant conventional citrus, such as satsuma mandarins and kumquats, can be grown in the ground with protection in areas just beyond the citrus belt—in the Florida panhandle, for example. Elsewhere in this region, hardy citrus (see pages 88–89) is more appropriate.

INDOOR/OUTDOOR REGION
Conventional varieties can be grown in pots and kept outdoors during warm weather, then moved indoors in winter; or they can be treated as year-round houseplants.

Ample sunshine and moderate temperatures all year round make this Southern California coastal valley an ideal locale for citrus. The aerial view shows commercial groves.

tive varieties suffer damage starting at 28°F/ −2°C—but only if the cold persists for several hours. A brief plunge to frostier levels may not be as injurious as prolonged exposure to moderate cold.

To find out how cold your garden gets, take readings with a minimum-maximum thermometer, which records the lowest as well as the highest and current temperatures. Don't go by the lows reported in the newspaper or on television: these figures may be for areas colder or warmer than your garden.

THE CITRUS BELT

The world's citrus-growing regions occupy a belt between approximately 40° north latitude and 40° south. Myriad varieties are cultivated in Central and South America, South Africa, the Mediterranean basin, the Middle East, India, China, Japan, Australia, and New Zealand.

In the United States, the citrus belt coincides pretty much with the U.S. Department of Agriculture (USDA) climate zones 9 and 10. When the USDA revised its map in 1990, it moved all zones a bit farther south to reflect changes in the weather: because of repeated freezes, the Florida panhandle and the coastal areas of Alabama and Mississippi were reassigned to zone 8. Home gardeners in these areas can still grow conventional citrus if they choose the most cold-tolerant varieties and provide winter protection.

Though the prime U.S. citrus-growing areas can be categorized as subtropical, their climates differ sharply. Conditions are humid in the Southeast and along the Gulf Coast, much drier in the West. On pages 12 and 13, we provide more specific information about each region, moving from west to east across the country.

California

Several mountain ranges and a long coastline of cold water have contributed to the many climates of California. Scores of citrus varieties thrive in the Mediterranean conditions of the coast and inland valleys, and in the more arid low desert. The main commercial citrus crops are oranges (especially navels), lemons, and grapefruit.

In all the state's citrus-growing areas, summers are warm and dry, though fog moderates heat and elevates humidity near the coast. Rain comes mainly from November to April, with little if any during the summer. Periodic hot, dry winds in inland and desert valleys can desiccate citrus quickly.

Many areas in Southern California and along the coast are normally frost-free, but all regions are subject to cold damage. The Central Valley is quite chilly in winter, though often a blanket of fog helps protect citrus trees.

Day and night temperatures fluctuate widely throughout California. The frigid Pacific Ocean causes the thermometer to dip at night in much of the state. The desert is cool after sundown, since the day's heat radiates quickly into the cloudless skies.

Arizona

Though citrus originated in the humid tropics, many types prosper in the low and intermediate deserts of Arizona. Summer days are intensely hot—so much so that citrus bark and fruit often sunburn—but nights are chilly after sundown. Hot winds can blow at any time.

The humidity level is extremely low most of the year, but it rises in summer, when tropical air rushes in from the Gulf of California. Isolated thunderstorms occur at that time; localized areas such as Tucson sometimes

Home gardeners in freeze-prone areas such as Texas are wise to select early-ripening varieties that can be harvested before the onset of frigid weather.

receive several inches of torrential rain, though the moisture dissipates rapidly.

The low desert is warm in winter, but temperatures occasionally drop low enough to damage citrus. Commercial groves are located here; the main crops are lemons, oranges, mandarins, and tangelos.

The intermediate desert is colder than the low desert and experiences more frequent freezes. Home gardeners here are well advised to choose hardy varieties and to plant them in sheltered locations.

Texas

This state has diverse climates, but only the hot, humid south and Gulf Coast areas are favorable for citrus. Regions too far inland are subject to repeated freezes, though the danger of damaging cold exists even near the Gulf.

Heavy freezes can occur as early as December, making early-ripening varieties a prudent choice. Tender citrus is best restricted to deep South Texas—roughly speaking, the region extending from the Lower Rio Grande Valley north to about Corpus Christi. Commercial groves are located here; though the industry began in the Houston-Beaumont area, freezes have forced it south. The main crop is grapefruit.

Cold-tolerant varieties can be grown in the freeze-prone area north of Corpus Christi. For details, see "Upper Gulf Coast" (below).

Texas citrus-growing areas are muggy all year. The Gulf waters keep nights warm, so daily temperatures fluctuate much less here than in the West. Rainfall is heaviest from May to September, but precipitation can occur any time. Periodic tropical storms with high winds can damage citrus trees.

Upper Gulf Coast

This region encompasses the Gulf Coast from north of Corpus Christi, Texas, through coastal Louisiana, Mississippi, and Alabama, and on into Florida (for information on north and west Florida, see below).

Sultry weather during most of the year is the defining feature of this region—but so is damaging winter cold. In fact, recurrent freezes during the 1980s virtually eliminated commercial citrus groves. Home gardeners will have the best chances of success with cold-tolerant varieties such as satsuma mandarins and kumquats.

Florida

Florida's prolonged heat and humidity provide an ideal environment for citrus. Some rain falls every month, with the largest amounts from June through September. Unstable air masses over the state in summer result in daily afternoon showers, and sometimes severe tropical storms. Thanks to the warm tropical waters, the air doesn't cool off much after sundown.

Winter cold is the limiting factor in growing citrus in north and west Florida: freezes are likely every year in these regions. Home gardeners north of about Gainesville are advised to grow the same sorts of cold-

Sour oranges (above) are suited to more regions of the citrus belt than blood oranges (top), which need daytime heat for sugars to form and chilly nights for rosy color to develop. Sour oranges prosper in cool or warm areas, where temperatures fluctuate a little or a lot.

tolerant varieties suitable for the upper Gulf Coast (see above left).

South of Gainesville, winters are considerably milder—the reason why the Florida citrus industry, which started in the St. Augustine area, has moved southward over the years. Many locales, especially in the southern tip of the state, are normally frost-free. However, periodic freezes do occur, generally in January or February. Sweet oranges and grapefruit are the main commercial citrus crops, but home gardeners can grow almost any variety.

'Minneola' tangelo (far left) typically forms a more prominent neck in arid climates than it does in more humid ones. A desert-grown 'Temple' tangor (left) has a thicker, more pebbly rind and a higher acid content than the same variety cultivated in Florida.

How Climate Affects Citrus

Heat and humidity give citrus a head start in many respects. In sultry regions, trees grow faster and start bearing at an earlier age than they do in drier or cooler areas. And flowering—the first step in the fruiting process—begins earlier in the season.

Once the fruit has formed, heat determines how fast it grows and how soon it ripens. That's why it's impossible to give a single harvest date, applicable to all regions, for any given citrus variety. Crops ripen fastest in Florida and South Texas, then in the Arizona and California deserts. Within California, the same variety matures first in the desert, then in inland valleys, and finally on the coast. Between the hottest climates and the coolest ones, ripening dates may differ by as much as several months.

Though fruit ripens later in cool regions, it hangs on the tree longer after maturity. Warm nights break down ripe fruit, making for a shorter harvest season in Florida than on the California coast.

Citrus fruit grows biggest in hot, humid regions, creating a problem for growers who end up with jumbo navel oranges and lemons. This shouldn't matter in a home garden—in fact, many gardeners take pride in producing oversized fruits and vegetables!

In humid climates, the fruit has a smoother, thinner peel and tends to be flatter in shape; where conditions are dry, it has a thicker, rougher skin and, often, a longer axis. Arid climates also tend to produce grapefruit with a pear shape, necked citrus varieties with a more obvious neck, and navel oranges with a more pronounced navel. Hot, humid conditions yield the juiciest fruit. An old joke among citrus scientists (in Florida, presumably) goes as follows: If you ran over a Florida orange with a car, you'd find a wet spot on the road, but if you ran over a California orange, you'd get dust.

Since acid content decreases more slowly during cool nights, citrus raised in California and Arizona has a more acidic component than it does in the Gulf Coast states. As a result, relatively high-acid varieties—'Temple' tangor, for example—are better suited to Florida than to California, where they may be too tart. On the other hand, California navel oranges have a complex, sweet-tart flavor compared to the very sweet navels grown in Florida.

Climate also influences the color of citrus fruit. Blood oranges color up when exposed to chilly nights during the ripening process, so they're well suited to inland California valleys but a bust in Florida. Pigmented grapefruit and pummelos have the reddest flesh in areas with the highest summer temperatures, though the color tends to fade in extreme desert heat; in cool-summer areas, though, the fruit looks white-fleshed.

Oranges, most mandarins, and lemons need cool temperatures while ripening to turn bright orange or yellow. Thus, the fruit has a green exterior and pale flesh in the tropics; and in Florida and Texas, it's greener on the outside and paler inside than it is in the West.

Growing a cold-sensitive citrus tree, such as this lemon, against a warm, sunny house wall with a roof overhang provides some protection in frost-prone areas.

DEALING WITH FREEZES

Cold weather severe enough to injure or kill citrus trees can strike any part of the citrus belt sooner or later. Potentially damaging freezes fall into two categories.

A radiation freeze, usually called a "frost" in California, occurs on a cold, calm, clear night when there is nothing to keep the warm air absorbed during the day from radiating back into the atmosphere. Most of the freezes in California, Arizona, and Florida are of this kind; they can be very local events.

The other type, sometimes called an advective freeze, is due to a cold air front. Typically, a wave of arctic air accompanied by winds sweeps down from the north and makes its way southward east of the Rockies, striking Texas and the upper Gulf Coast more often than Florida. Such fronts seldom move westward.

To take suitable action, commercial growers need to know the type of freeze they're up against. For example, while wind machines are effective in mixing the cold and warm air layers that form in a radiation freeze, they're useless in fighting a windy cold front.

For home gardeners, who don't have access to special equipment and usually only have one or a few trees to protect, identifying the kind of freeze isn't important: the same measures can be used in either case. Protection pays—even if your citrus doesn't entirely escape the effects of a freeze, it can usually recover from slight damage within a year.

Long-term Measures

If you live in a freeze-prone area, take these steps to avoid losing fruit and to give your trees a better chance of survival.

■ Choose cold-tolerant varieties.

■ Select hardy rootstocks; some are more cold-resistant than others.

■ Opt for early ripeners, such as satsuma mandarins and navel oranges, so you can harvest before cold weather arrives.

■ Plant in a protected location and avoid low spots (see "Taking Advantage of Micro-climates," page 17).

■ Install screens or buffers to mitigate persistent winds.

■ Start fertilizing only after the last spring frost and stop in late summer; in this way, you'll avoid stimulating new growth that is vulnerable to cold.

Freeze-fighting measures include wrapping the trunk in an insulating material (top), and covering the tree and raising the temperature around it with trouble lights (above).

■ Don't prune in fall or winter: that may stimulate tender new growth.

■ Keep trees well irrigated and as healthy as possible, since stressed plants are more susceptible to freeze damage.

■ If freezes are frequent and severe, plant in containers that can be sheltered.

Short-term Measures

Be prepared to take immediate action when a freeze is predicted.

■ Water the soil a day or two before the freeze and again once it hits. Moist soil holds more heat than dry soil, and the water itself will release heat as it cools and freezes. Don't sprinkle the whole tree; ice may form and cause branches to break.

■ Expose the bare soil over the root zone, since it absorbs more heat than mulch, weeds, or other coverings.

■ Wrap the trunk in an insulating material, such as heavy corrugated cardboard, several layers of newspapers, batting, or cornstalks. A soil bank (a mound of soil around the trunk) insulates best of all, though it can lead to insect and disease problems if not completely removed after the freeze.

■ If the tree is small enough, build a protective frame and cover it with cloth or plastic. Encasing the tree isn't necessary; a top cover alone is fine, but make sure it doesn't touch the tree. Permeable covers can be left in place until the freeze is over, but plastic should be removed during the day.

■ Raise the temperature around the tree with a couple of 150-watt light bulbs, floodlights, trouble lights, a heat lamp, or a small electric heater. Even Christmas lights hung in the tree will add some warmth.

■ Don't delay in moving potted trees to protection, since roots in containers aren't as well insulated as those in the ground.

Taking Advantage of Microclimates

Even if the general climate in your area isn't ideal for growing certain types of citrus, you may be able to succeed by planting in favorable microclimates. These are the little climates on your property—the hot spots, cool locations, humid areas, and so on. Microclimates change seasonally and over time as plants grow—so get to know your garden.

A wind-protected, warm, sunny microclimate is ideal for citrus. Anything less than full sunlight results in willowy growth and poor fruiting. If you need more warmth, plant against a light-colored, sunny wall, preferably near paving. (Remember, southern exposures are generally the warmest, followed by western, eastern, and northern—though western exposures are the hottest in summer at the lower latitudes, such as in deep South Texas and Florida.) If you have such a planting spot, you may be able to grow grapefruit or other heat-demanding varieties, even if these won't succeed for your neighbors.

If too much heat or sunburn is the problem, locate your trees under overhangs or in spots that get part shade at midday. Avoid south- and west-facing walls and areas where much of the ground is covered by asphalt or concrete.

In freeze-prone climates, a well-chosen microclimate can keep trees a few degrees warmer in winter. Choose a spot against a sunny wall, for example; an area beneath eaves or other overhangs is good too, as long as the tree is exposed to sun. You can also plant on a gentle slope, since cold air flows downhill and collects at the bottom. Protect citrus from gales by planting downwind of more wind-tolerant trees or by erecting a barrier.

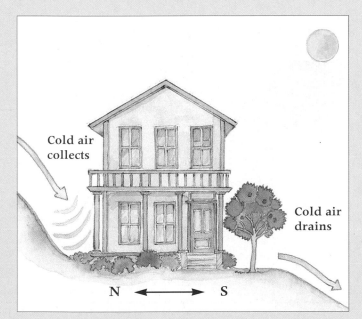

The citrus tree is planted on the sunny side of the house, away from spots where cold air collects.

Heat from the sun is reflected from the house wall, bare soil, and pavement onto the citrus tree.

CITRUS IN THE LANDSCAPE

Citrus trees are more than just fruit factories: they're ornamentals deserving of a prominent place in the landscape. Whether grown in the ground or raised in pots, these plants belong on show—in borders, at entryways, poolside, as a focal point in the front yard, or in any other place where their evergreen foliage, fragrant blooms, and colorful fruit can be admired and appreciated.

A lemon tree is grown as an informal espalier against a terra-cotta wall.

Centuries ago, citrus trees were often used as decorative borders for other plantings. Once the fruits became important crops, however, the trees were relegated to groves and their ornamental qualities were largely forgotten. Unfortunately, many home gardeners still think of citrus as orchard trees, not realizing how beautifully they can adorn the landscape. But as the photos in this chapter show, these plants can quite easily be integrated into your garden, providing lovely elements in the overall design. They play a wide range of roles, serving as—among other possibilities—specimen or shade trees, foundation or poolside plants, screens, hedges, thorny barriers, espaliers, arbor coverings, and decorations for patios and decks.

Citrus trees can also be incorporated into mixed borders with perennials and ground covers. Since citrus is so shallow-rooted, any plantings over the root zone should be permanent. Ideally, choose ground covers that spread out without putting down roots.

When you want citrus to stand out in your landscape, choose types with especially eye-catching features. For example, consider the myrtlelike foliage of 'Chinotto' sour orange; the heady perfume and graceful umbrella shape of 'Bouquet de Fleurs', another sour orange; the rosy-skinned fruit of 'Sanguinelli' blood orange; the green-and-white foliage of variegated calamondin; and the contorted branches and curved thorns of 'Flying Dragon' trifoliate orange.

Don't forget the way citrus trees brighten the garden in fall and winter, when color is

Arcs of herbs and potted lemon trees radiate from a central patio in this Portland, Oregon, garden. The citrus can be carried to shelter when the weather turns frosty.

especially welcome. Instead of stringing conifers or other plants with lights to turn them into living Christmas trees, you can let citrus transform itself. Some types, including sour orange, kumquat, orangequat, 'Rangpur' sour-acid mandarin, and calamondin, produce brilliant (and edible) ornaments that hang on the tree for up to a year.

Left: A 'Eureka' lemon tree gives permanent structure to this herbaceous border. Above: Planted in a backyard corner, an orange tree creates a privacy screen.

Below: A lemon tree ringed with flowering ground covers softens a stark concrete walkway. Bottom: A row of informally espaliered citrus trees includes kumquat, lemon, lime, and orange.

This page, clockwise from near right: 'Eureka' lemon fence, located in the Sunset courtyard and espaliered in a horizontal cordon pattern, is more than 40 years old; potted dwarf mandarin is underplanted with baby's tears; and handsome 'Marsh' grapefruit tree in a garden border bears both new and old crop.

This page, clockwise from top left: Lemon trees screen the steep yard from the street; 'Dancy' mandarin tree, pruned into a globe, anchors a bed of colorful annuals and perennials; citrus trees with Johnny-jump-ups at their bases alternate with pink tulips in a poolside container planting; and a 'Valencia' orange tree decorates the front entryway.

Citrus Espaliers

Classic espalier was developed by 16th- and 17th-century European master gardeners. Looking for a way to grow fruit trees in confined areas, they hit upon the idea of training the branches into a flat framework.

Space limitations still offer a good reason to espalier. But this technique has other advantages besides letting you produce lemons or oranges in a narrow bed or side yard. Training the tree against a warm, sunny wall may supply enough heat for fruit ripening or winter survival in a chancy climate. An espalier also dresses up a plain fence or wall.

Just about any type of standard or dwarf citrus can be espaliered, though certain varieties are particularly suitable because of vining branches or an open growth habit. Among the best choices are 'Eureka' and 'Ponderosa' lemons, 'Nagami' kumquat, 'Eustis' limequat, 'Tarocco' blood orange, and 'Chandler' pummelo. It's best to start with a young tree rather than trying to transform a mature one.

Espalier Patterns

If you're a novice gardener or have little time for pruning, an informal fan is the easiest espalier for you. There's no precise pattern; you just plant the tree directly in front of a structure, allow it to branch naturally, and remove any growth that sticks out too far.

A formal espalier requires more attention and patience. Here, you train the tree into a precise geometric pattern, such as a horizontal cordon (below) or a candelabra, double U-shape, or palmette (see opposite page). For a somewhat more casual look, choose a so-called random pattern (also shown opposite). If a standard design doesn't appeal to you, develop one of your own. Regardless of the pattern, space the rows at least 18 inches apart: if they're any closer, the design will be obscured, since you must let the foliage grow in thickly for good fruiting.

CREATING A HORIZONTAL CORDON

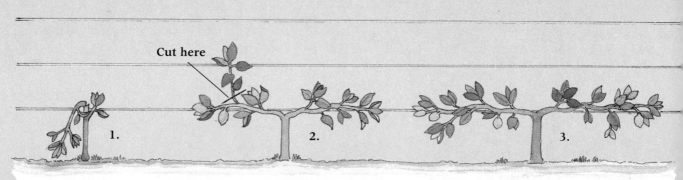

Cut here

1. 2. 3.

1. To start branching lower, cut partway through the trunk above the desired height for the first cordon. Push the top over, then remove it after the new shoots appear.

2. Select the strongest shoots and train them along the wire. Prune off excess growth that doesn't fit the pattern.

3. As the horizontal growth matures, the branch tips tend to droop and hang down for fruiting. Let them sag, and select the most vigorous upward-growing side shoots to continue along the wire.

Before deciding on a pattern, remember that working with nature is easier than fighting it. If the tree is naturally upright, choose an upright pattern; if the branches tend to be horizontal, opt for that type of design.

To cover a large area, repeat the pattern. Such a repetition of a 'Eureka' lemon horizontal cordon forms a living fence in the *Sunset* courtyard (see page 24). Free-standing espaliers such as this one can be trained on 12- to 14-gauge galvanized wire stretched between 4-by-4 posts. A wooden trellis set into the ground is another good support; you can even espalier a potted citrus tree if you attach the trellis to the container.

You may want to espalier against an existing structure, such as a fence or house wall. Train the branches on wires pulled taut between eyescrews or bolts set into the wood or masonry. For air circulation, keep the wires 8 to 12 inches away from the structure.

ESPALIER PATTERNS

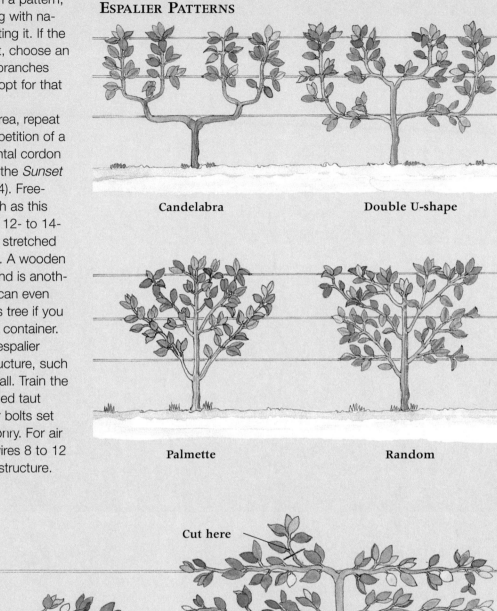

Candelabra

Double U-shape

Palmette

Random

Cut here

4.

5.

4. Start the next cordon after the first has grown to the desired size. Let a strong shoot from the trunk or the middle of the first cordon grow upward, then pinch it back at the second wire to force side shoots. Train as for the first cordon.

5. Repeat the process for additional cordons. Continue to prune wayward growth after the espalier is established.

SELECTING & PLANTING CITRUS

Which citrus will you get? 'Valencia' orange, 'Minneola' tangelo, satsuma mandarin, 'Improved Meyer' lemon... the choices go on and on. Look to this chapter for help in deciding on just the right variety and in choosing a healthy specimen. A simple guide to budding citrus is provided as well, in case you can't locate the tree you want and you're willing to try your hand at propagation. Finally, we give instructions for planting citrus in the ground and in pots.

'Chinotto' sour orange was chosen for its compact size, myrtlelike leaves, and the colorful fruit that hangs on the tree for up to a year.

ANATOMY OF A CITRUS TREE

The category of plants we refer to as citrus includes many types of evergreen (except for the deciduous trifoliate orange), usually thorny, small to medium-size trees.

Most commercially marketed citrus trees consist of two parts. The *scion* is the upper part of the tree, which produces the desirable fruit; the *rootstock* is the lower few inches of the trunk and the roots. Scion and rootstock are joined at the *bud union*. On a young tree, the union is conspicuous as a cut area at a dogleg bend in the trunk. The bend disappears within a few years, though the contrast between the two barks is evident for much longer.

It's natural to wonder why such two-part plants are favored over all-of-a-piece citrus. By grafting mature fruiting wood onto a rootstock, growers can produce plants that start bearing fruit in just a few years, compared to 10 to 15 years for seedling trees. The rootstock is chosen not only for its compatibility with the scion, but also for suitability to local soil conditions, disease resistance, and—in freeze-prone areas—cold hardiness. Certain rootstocks may be favored because of their

effect on the fruit quality and productivity of some varieties.

Citrus is noted for its thick, leathery leaves and white or purplish, often fragrant blossoms. The fruit of all types—despite the wide variety in appearance and flavor—is a *hesperidium,* a berry with a leathery rind and segmented, typically juicy flesh.

A citrus tree usually goes through several yearly growth flushes, each capable of producing flowers and setting fruit. In most varieties, only the initial spring flush is productive, and the tree yields a single crop in fall or winter. Everbearing types, including lemons, limes, citrons, and calamondin, can bloom and set fruit throughout the year, though they do so most heavily in spring. Citrus fruit ripens only on the tree and should be left there until it reaches maximum sweetness or juiciness.

Citrus grows most actively between 70°F/21°C and 90°F/32°C; it stops growing when temperatures exceed 100°F/38°C or drop below 55°F/13°C. The slowdown in winter approaches dormancy, though citrus trees aren't truly dormant in the way deciduous plants are.

The ultimate size of the plant depends on the variety. For example, mandarins generally reach 10 to 20 feet tall and grapefruit about

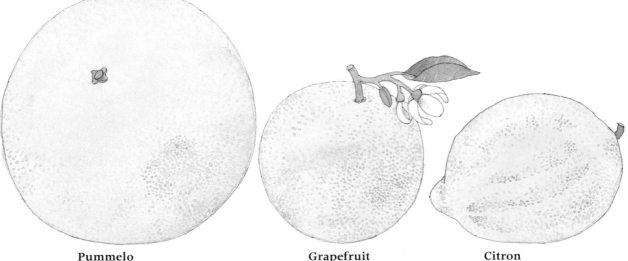

Pummelo   **Grapefruit**   **Citron**

30 feet. Varieties within a category may differ: among sour oranges, for instance, 'Seville' stretches upright to 20 to 30 feet, while 'Bouquet de Fleurs' is a spreading tree growing just 8 to 10 feet high.

Growing conditions also influence tree size. In a home garden, crowding and root competition often impede growth. Trees raised in containers are naturally dwarfed, since their roots are restricted. Other factors affecting size include climate and amount of sun or shade: citrus grows larger in warm, humid areas than in dry or cool regions, and trees are lankier in shade than in sun. Availability of water and nutrients is important as well; trees are stunted when starved for either.

Standard versus Dwarf

A standard tree attains the full size typical for the variety; a dwarf grows on a rootstock that reduces the proportions of the tree, though not of the fruit.

Dwarf citrus was first developed in California, where it remains extremely popular. Many dwarf plants are also available in Arizona and through mail-order suppliers (located in various states) who sell them for container culture.

Whether a tree is actually a dwarf is sometimes unclear, since no rules govern the use of

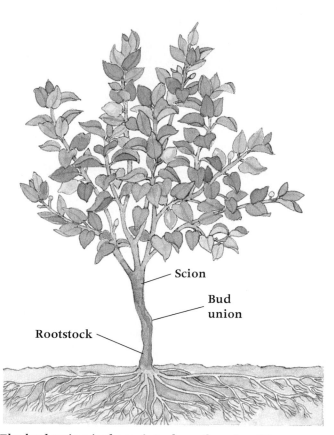

Scion

Bud union

Rootstock

The bud union is the point where the scion (the desirable fruiting variety) is joined to the rootstock.

the term. Some trees sold as dwarfs will ultimately reach standard size. To make sure you really are getting a dwarf, deal with a reputable nursery, preferably one that can provide information about the rootstock.

The only true genetic dwarf rootstock is 'Flying Dragon' ('Hirya' in Japanese), a mutation of trifoliate orange. Varieties grafted onto it reach about half the size they would as

Navel orange   Lemon   Mandarin   Calamondin   Kumquat

Sex Life of Citrus

Most citrus is self-pollinating, producing bountiful crops even when a single tree is planted in isolation. Of all citrus, only a few mandarin types require another variety nearby for pollination. And some kinds, such as satsuma mandarins and navel oranges, set fruit even when the flower isn't fertilized; the resulting fruit is seedless.

The many citrus types are thought to have originated from just two or three ancestors. But as hybridizers discovered in the early 1900s, the breeding that occurred in nature is not so easy to duplicate in the laboratory.

A phenomenon called *nucellar embryony* put the brakes on breeding. Most citrus produce two types of embryos in the same seed—vegetative embryos from a part of the seed called the nucellus, and sexual ones from the union of egg and pollen. The vegetative embryos outcompete the sexual ones and develop into seedlings identical to the mother plant.

When early breeders tried to hybridize oranges and grapefruit, they kept ending up with clones. They therefore concentrated on using the few non-nucellar types, such as kumquats, pummelos, and certain mandarins, as seed parents. This resulted in new classes of citrus such as tangelos, limequats, and orangequats; more recently, grapefruit-pummelo hybrids have been produced from such crosses.

For a sense of how complicated citrus genealogy is, consider what supposedly happened when Florida citrus scientists sowed seeds of the non-nucellar 'Persian' lime, itself a hybrid between a lime and a lemon or citron, in hopes of getting an improved strain. First they had to find seeds of the basically seedless variety, which they did by sifting through several dump-truck loads of lime pulp. From the 250 or so seedlings thus obtained, they identified sweet orange, sour orange, grapefruit, lemon, mandarin, limequat, and citron—and only two 'Persian' lime trees.

standard trees. This is the one rootstock that many growers in California consider important enough to label by name.

Several other rootstocks have a dwarfing effect on certain fruiting varieties. The resulting tree, often labeled "semidwarf," typically grows about two-thirds the standard size.

Nearly all citrus varieties sold in California are available dwarfed to some extent. The notable exception is true lemon ('Eureka' and 'Lisbon'), which is too vigorous for dwarfing.

DECIDING ON A VARIETY

Climate is a key factor in choosing the right variety for your garden, since citrus types differ in the amount of heat they need and cold they will tolerate. In cool-summer, mild-winter San Francisco, you're better off with lemons than grapefruit; in warm-summer, freeze-prone North Florida, satsuma mandarins are more suitable than sweet oranges. For more about the climatic needs of citrus, consult "Where Citrus Grows" (pages 7–17) and the encyclopedia beginning on page 63.

Citrus trees come in many sizes and shapes, so consider the role you want the plant to fulfill in the landscape. You might choose one type for a specimen tree, another for a small foundation plant, and yet another for a fruiting hedge. If your goal is a home orchard, however, proportions don't really matter.

In many parts of the citrus belt, you can harvest fresh fruit most of the year if you select varieties that ripen at different times. In freeze-prone areas, it's important to choose early ripeners.

Of course, there's no point in growing a variety that fits all your parameters unless you like the fruit. Even if you garden in prime grapefruit-growing country, why culti-

Different forms of the same citrus variety are illustrated above. Standard trees are the norm in Florida, Texas, and along the Gulf Coast. In the West, citrus is also available on dwarfing rootstocks. All types can be espaliered.

vate that fruit if you prefer oranges? If a seedy fruit bothers you, choose a variety with few to no seeds. You may want to sample certain varieties before making up your mind. Look for tastings at nurseries; check specialty markets for unusual citrus fruits.

In the end, availability may dictate your decision. Though there are many hundreds of named varieties of citrus around the world, you don't have access to the entire inventory.

Because the citrus-producing states prohibit importation of citrus plants, home gardeners living in these regions must buy from locally grown stocks. Local nurseries typically offer a few to a few dozen of the most popular and suitable varieties for the climate, and they can usually special-order additional kinds. If you're willing to try propagating your own citrus, you can expand your options by obtaining stock from a grower or a budwood program (see pages 35–36).

Outside the citrus states, gardeners must rely on mail-order suppliers. These companies

Multiple-variety Trees

Though most citrus trees sold consist of a single fruiting variety, it's possible to graft several kinds onto the same tree. Such plants, sometimes called "fruit cocktail" trees, may appeal to you if you like novelty specimens or if you want to raise several types of citrus in a very small yard. Be aware that the trees tend to look a little unbalanced and gangly, since each variety grows at a different rate.

You can purchase a multiple-variety tree or bud additional varieties onto an existing citrus tree in your yard. For budding, follow the basic instructions on page 35, but insert the buds higher up on the tree and try to match the diameter of the budwood to the limb. It's a good idea to dab bright paint at the base of each budded shoot, so you don't accidentally prune it off later.

Sweet orange, mandarin, tangelo, grapefruit, kumquat, and calamondin can all be used interchangeably as budwood and stock trees. Neither 'Eureka' nor 'Lisbon' lemon is satisfactory for budding onto; these varieties are best left as single trees.

Where to See Citrus

If you live near Winter Haven, Florida, or Riverside, California (or if you are in the vicinity at the right time), you have a chance to view many varieties of citrus. Late fall through spring is the best time to see ripe fruit on the trees.

The 6½-acre Florida Citrus Arboretum, established in 1975, contains more than 250 citrus varieties from around the world. It is located at 3027 Lake Alfred Road, Winter Haven; for information, call (941) 294-4267.

California Citrus State Historic Park is a new facility which will eventually replicate an old-time citrus-producing community. A collection of 80 citrus varieties has already been planted; the trees should begin full production in the late 1990s. The park is located on Van Buren Boulevard at Dufferin Avenue, Riverside. For information, call (909) 780-6222.

This is how the Florida Citrus Arboretum looked shortly after it was established.

carry a fairly limited selection of conventional citrus varieties for container growing; some also sell hardy citrus for planting in the ground.

BUYING A CITRUS TREE

When purchasing any fruit tree, deal with a reputable supplier, so you can be confident you're getting a healthy specimen of the variety listed on the label.

The plant label should precisely identify the fruiting variety. Just "lemon," for example, is not enough; look for the specific kind, such as 'Improved Meyer' or 'Eureka'. In Florida, labeling for both scion and rootstock is required by law. In other states, you don't know what rootstock you're getting, though knowledgeable nursery personnel should be able to tell you.

Unlike many other plants, citrus tends to be sold by common rather than botanical name. For example, you'll usually see 'Kinnow' mandarin or 'Meiwa' kumquat, not Citrus reticulata 'Kinnow' or Fortunella crassifolia 'Meiwa'.

Depending on the source, mail-order citrus comes bare-root or potted, and in a range of sizes. Since you can't choose the tree in person, you have to rely on the supplier for a good-quality plant.

Citrus trees sold in nurseries and garden centers are usually available in 5-, 7-, and 15-gallon containers, and occasionally in 1- and 2-gallon cans. You may be drawn to the largest specimens, since a good-sized tree makes an immediate impact, especially if it's loaded with flowers and fruit. But bear in mind that younger trees that haven't begun to bear transplant better—and they cost less, too.

Pick a healthy-looking plant with good foliage color, no obvious pest damage, and no nicks in the bark. The bud union should be smooth and positioned well above soil level to lessen the danger of rot. The straighter the trunk, the better. Also look for a strong trunk, so the tree won't need staking. Any branching should be fairly symmetrical. Avoid plants with roots that protrude from the container or are tightly coiled around the root ball.

BUDDING A CITRUS TREE

Why propagate your own citrus tree if you can buy one at the nursery? One reason lies in that "if": the nursery may not have the variety you're after. Or you may want to rework a freeze-damaged tree that is now putting up suckers from the rootstock.

Simply put, budding consists of taking a bud from one citrus tree and inserting it under the bark of another so that it will take hold and grow.

If you're starting from scratch, you need both budwood (a twig with buds along its length) and a rootstock. State budwood programs (see page 36) are a good source of budwood; you may also be able to buy budwood from an agreeable nursery or grower. A nursery or grower can probably also supply you with seedlings for the rootstock; get a recommendation for an appropriate rootstock when you order the budwood.

If you're grafting onto an existing rootstock, you'll need just budwood. Knowing the type of rootstock is important, since you need to choose a compatible scion. If no one can identify the rootstock (the previous fruiting variety may provide a clue), you can always experiment and see what takes.

For directions on budding, see the illustrations at right. Remember, bud only when the

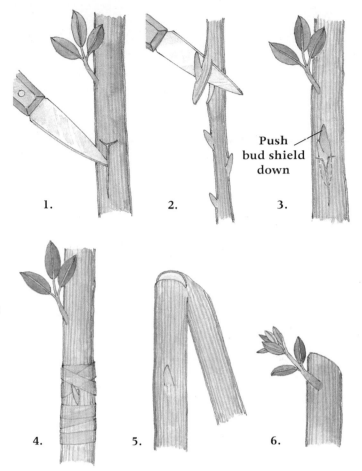

1. **2.** **Push bud shield down** **3.**

4. **5.** **6.**

1. With a sharp knife, make a vertical cut 1 to 1½ inches long through the bark to the wood. Make a horizontal cut about ½ inch long to form either an upright or inverted "T."

2. Holding the knife almost parallel to the budwood, slice off a bud with a sliver of wood extending about ½ inch below and above the bud.

3. Push the bud shield under the flaps of the "T," making sure the bud faces up. If any part of the shield protrudes, cut it off.

4. Wrap the two parts with budding tape, florist's tape, or clear polyethylene (not vinyl) plastic. Overlap the tape, but don't cover the bud itself.

5. Remove the tape after the pieces of wood have united, usually in a few weeks. Cut about three-fourths of the way through the rootstock, on the same side as the bud and about 2 inches above it; push the top part over.

6. Cut off the rootstock top after the bud has grown several inches, making a sloping cut about ½ inch above the bud.

Budwood Programs

The major citrus-growing states operate programs to safeguard citrus varieties and to test new varieties before releasing budwood to growers. Though industry-oriented, the state programs will sell budwood to home gardeners within their borders; minimum orders are usually required.

Typically pencil-diameter and containing several buds, the budwood you purchase is certified to be disease-free and true to type for that variety. For specifics on available varieties and prices, contact your state program.

ARIZONA
University of Arizona
Yuma Mesa Agricultural
  Center
RR1, Box 40M
Somerton, AZ 85350
Tel: (502) 726-0458
Both budwood and root-
stock seeds or seedlings
are available.

CALIFORNIA
Citrus Clonal Protection
  Program
Department of Plant Pathology
University of California
Riverside, CA 92521
Fax (no calls, please):
(909) 686-5612
Budwood is available.

FLORIDA
Citrus Budwood
  Registration Bureau
3027 Lake Alfred Road
Winter Haven, FL 33881
Tel: (941) 294-4267
Budwood and occasionally
rootstock seeds are avail-
able to home gardeners in
Florida as well as outside
the citrus belt.

TEXAS
Texas Citrus Budwood
  Program
Texas A&M-Kingsville
  Citrus Center
P.O. Box 1150
Weslaco, TX 78596
Tel: (210) 968-2132
Fax: (210) 969-0649
Budwood for a limited number
of varieties is available; the
selection will expand along
with the newly inaugurated
program.

tree is actively growing and the bark is slipping—that is, when it's loose enough to peel back when you cut into it. This usually occurs between April and September. To avoid rot problems, always bud at least several inches above soil level.

PLANTING IN THE GROUND

Citrus trees can be grown in the ground wherever the climate permits. The plants tolerate a wide range of soils, from sandy types to clay, and accept pH levels from slightly acid to fairly alkaline (approximately pH 5.5 to 8.0).

Good drainage is essential, since citrus trees don't tolerate standing water. If you don't know whether your soil drains adequately, test it. Dig a 2-foot-deep hole of any width and fill it with water; let the water soak in completely, then refill the hole and note the drop in the water level. If it sinks less than 6 inches in a 24-hour period, the drainage is poor.

To improve drainage in heavy clay soil, work in plenty of organic matter. If the problem is compacted soil (as around a new homesite), you can hire a landscape contractor to loosen it. If a soil pan—an impenetrable layer beneath the surface—is impeding drainage, try breaking through it; you may succeed if the layer is thin enough. Dealing with boggy soil may mean installing drain lines.

If you can't solve the drainage problem fairly easily, then grow citrus in raised beds filled with good soil. The beds needn't be too deep, since citrus is very shallow-rooted; even old trees have most of their roots in the top 2 feet of soil. If you live in an area where the water table is high or where heavy rains are likely, plant on a slight mound.

Where to Plant

Any warm, sunny spot sheltered from the wind is suitable for citrus. If you're trying to beat the heat or cold, take advantage of your garden's microclimates (see page 17).

Always allot enough room for the tree to grow to its ultimate size. A standard-size sweet orange tree, for example, will eventual-

When growing citrus in lawn, remove a large circle of grass beneath the trees, as shown above. In chancy climates, choose a more protected spot; for example, the orange trees at right are planted near the house wall.

ly occupy a space 20 to 25 feet high and wide. Citrus roots extend beyond the canopy, so keep your citrus trees away from plants with aggressive root systems that will compete for water and nutrients. Also consider proximity to buildings, unless you are planning to espalier.

When planting in a lawn, remove grass in a 3- to 5-foot circle, both to cut down on competition from grass roots and to eliminate the risk of a lawnmower nicking the tree trunk. (In the dry-summer West, it's best to keep citrus out of lawns, since irrigating the trees on the same schedule as the grass can lead to rot diseases.)

When to Plant

The planting timetable depends on climate. Your goal is to give the roots the longest possible period to become established before extremes of temperature put the tree under stress.

In freeze-prone areas, plant in late winter or early spring, after all danger of frost is past; this will give the tree a full season in the ground before it's exposed to cold. In very hot-summer areas such as the desert, fall planting is a good idea; the tree will then be established before scorching weather arrives. You can also plant during autumn in normally frost-free regions. Fall planting in coastal California carries a nice bonus: the winter rains provide free watering.

How to Plant

Dig a hole no deeper than the root ball and about twice as wide. It's best not to create a richer environment in the hole by amending the backfill, since you want the roots to grow into the surrounding soil. In clay soil, rough up the sides of the hole to let the roots grow out more easily. Don't mix in fertilizer or place it at the bottom of the hole. Feed the tree only when it starts to produce new growth.

Proper planting gets a citrus tree off to a healthy start. Dig the planting hole no deeper than the root ball and approximately twice as wide, then place the tree in the hole and pack soil around the root ball. For easy watering, form a walled basin over the root zone.

Carefully remove the tree from its container; don't yank it out by the trunk. Wash off an inch or more of the soil mix all around the root ball so the roots will be in direct contact with the soil. Straighten out any circling roots; cut off any broken ones.

Plant the tree at the same level as (or up to an inch higher than) it grew in the container; the color demarcation on the trunk tells you where the previous soil level was. It's fine if a few upper roots are visible aboveground. Pack soil gently around the root ball, eliminating air pockets. When the hole is half full, fill it with water to settle the soil. Once the water has soaked in, pack in soil to the top; then water again.

A watering basin makes it easy to irrigate the newly planted tree. Use garden soil to form a continuous wall about 6 inches high and wide around the tree. Start with a diameter a little beyond the canopy, then enlarge it as the tree grows. If the tree is budded low, you can form an inner wall to ensure that water stays away from the trunk; the finished basin will have a doughnut shape. Immediately after planting the tree, drench the basin several times.

PLANTING IN CONTAINERS

If climate problems, poor soil, or lack of space prevent you from planting citrus in the ground, you can grow your trees in containers. Potted citrus is also a great choice for decks and patios.

In regions experiencing hard freezes, citrus trees can be grown as indoor-outdoor plants. During cold snaps, bring them indoors to a basement area or garage with good bright light.

Both standard and dwarf citrus trees are suitable for container culture. Remember that,

Citrus as a Houseplant

As an indoor plant, citrus performs best in a greenhouse or conservatory, but it can be grown under ordinary house conditions if placed near a bright south-facing window. There's no guarantee, however, that a tree will flower or fruit.

Sour-fruited varieties offer the best chances for good fruit, since they have a low heat requirement. Among the most popular choices are 'Improved Meyer' and 'Ponderosa' lemons, 'Bearss' or 'Persian' lime, kumquats, calamondin, and 'Rangpur' sour-acid mandarin. Sour oranges are less likely to produce a crop indoors.

Normally sweet citrus (navel oranges, for example) tends to be bitter when grown indoors, but it can always be used as a flavoring or for marmalade.

For information on caring for indoor citrus, see page 49.

'Nagami' kumquat is a popular choice for year-round indoor growing.

because roots are restricted, plants raised in pots are smaller than they would be if grown in the ground.

Some citrus, such as calamondin and 'Chinotto' sour orange, thrive in pots as small as 8 or 10 inches in diameter. In general, though, start with a container at least 18 inches across; this size should be ample for several years. The container can be made of wood (half whisky or wine barrels are ideal), clay, ceramic, or plastic.

Keep in mind that moisture evaporates faster from porous pots than nonporous ones, necessitating more frequent watering. If the pot doesn't have drainage holes, drill some in the bottom. A wheeled base makes it easy to move the plant to protection during cold weather. You can also move heavy pots from place to place with the aid of a dolly.

Plant in a light, well-drained soil mix; sterile sorts are an excellent choice, since they're free of pests and diseases. As when planting in the ground, don't mix any fertilizer into the soil and set the tree at the level it grew in the original pot. Allow 2 or 3 free inches at the top of the container for water. Firm the soil well around the root ball; then water thoroughly.

CARING FOR CITRUS

Treat your citrus tree right, and it will reward you with strong, healthy growth and good-quality fruit. Above all, proper care means consistent watering and fertilizing. This chapter offers advice not only on those two crucial tasks, but on weeding, mulching, pruning, and harvesting as well. You'll also find valuable tips on caring for container-grown citrus, both indoors and out.

Periodic pruning neatens the grapefruit and tangelo trees trained onto this arbor.

WATERING

A citrus tree needs moist but not sodden soil. It won't last long if you grow it in a bog. Nor will it flourish if soil is too dry: if you give it insufficient moisture in the root zone or let it go too long between waterings, it will retaliate by dropping leaves, blossoms, and fruit.

Since citrus is evergreen, it needs water all year. The demand is greatest when the trees are growing actively, usually from late winter or early spring through summer; the critical period is from the year's initial growth flush until the young fruit is at least an inch across.

Watering frequency is largely determined by climate. In the humid subtropics, rain handles the job to a certain degree. Normal rainfall in deep South Texas provides some water for citrus trees, but supplemental irrigation is a must. In areas farther north along the Gulf Coast, rainfall increases, though occasional watering is still necessary. In Florida, home gardeners can put away the hose in summer, but they may have to water during the rest of the year. In the more arid citrus-growing regions of California and Arizona, trees must be irrigated throughout the long dry season; from fall into spring, rain may provide some relief, depending on the locality.

After you water a plant, the moisture is depleted in two ways. It's absorbed by the roots and transpired through the leaves, and it also evaporates from the soil. The hotter, drier, or windier the conditions, the more rapid the depletion and, correspondingly, the greater the demand for water. In cooler, more

For basin flooding (below), use a hose to fill the basin, then let the water soak in. For drip irrigation (at right), position emitters over the root zone at the tree's dripline. Expand the watering area as the tree grows—make a larger basin or move the drip emitters farther out.

humid, or calmer weather, on the other hand, the rate of depletion slows and watering is required less frequently.

Other factors enter into the watering equation. Mulch has an effect: a layer over the root zone slows evaporation. Soil type is important. The sandier the soil, the more often your trees need water; the greater the clay content, the less often you need to irrigate. Trees in containers must be watered more often than those in the ground. A mature tree with extensive roots needs more water to wet the root zone thoroughly than does a young tree with a smaller root mass—but the smaller root system dries out faster, requiring more frequent watering.

All these variables make it difficult to provide precise figures on how much and how often to water. Though you may be tempted to establish a set schedule—say, once a week in light, well-drained soil and every 2 to 3 weeks in heavy soil—it's best simply to give

your tree water when it needs it. As a general rule, water when the top few inches of soil are dry but the rest of the root zone is still slightly moist. To detect moisture, stick your finger in the soil or use a moisture meter.

Watering Methods

Choose a technique that delivers water efficiently to the root system and keeps the trunk and bud union dry. Two excellent watering methods are basin flooding and drip irrigation.

Basin Flooding This method is pretty much limited to level sites, since it involves flooding a basin that you form over the root zone. A doughnut-shaped trough (see the illustration on page 38) keeps water away from a low bud union. You can do away with the inner wall of the basin if the tree is budded high and your soil is fast-draining.

Even if the tree is located in lawn, you'll want a basin so that you can flood the root system every month or so. Lawn sprinklers may do a good job of watering grass roots, which typically grow about 6 inches down, but they can't be trusted to provide adequate moisture for tree roots.

Drip Irrigation This term refers to any system that dispenses water slowly; the output is figured in gallons per hour (not in gallons per minute, as it is for lawn sprinklers). The technology includes minisprayers and minisprinklers in addition to drip emitters. Soaker hoses (rubber hoses with tiny holes along the surface) are often considered drip irrigation equipment.

Perhaps the most carefree drip system is one with in-line emitters already embedded inside the tubing, at intervals of 12, 18, 24, or 36 inches. To wet the entire root zone, place the hose containing the clogproof emitters in a ring around the tree at the dripline.

A local irrigation supplier can sell you the components for a drip system; some mail-order nurseries also carry kits.

FERTILIZING

Citrus trees need fairly large amounts of the three primary nutrients—nitrogen, phosphorus, and potassium—plus smaller amounts of ten other nutrients. Any deficiencies will show up in symptoms such as yellowed leaves, leaf or fruit drop, and so on (see the chart on pages 60–61).

Nitrogen is the nutrient that home gardeners everywhere must supply regularly: plants use it up quickly, and water from rainfall or irrigation rapidly washes it out of the soil. For plants growing in clay or loam, phosphorus and potassium need not be replenished as often, since they don't leach from the soil as readily. Sandy soils, however, are a different story. They're extremely poor at holding nutrients—so if your tree is growing in such a soil, plan on regularly providing phosphorus and potassium as well as nitrogen.

Most home citrus-growers use packaged fertilizers (see at right). If you want to use organic materials such as decomposed garden compost or well-rotted manure, keep in mind that applying them to citrus can cause problems: because you have to work large amounts into the soil, you may wind up damaging your tree's surface roots. It's probably safer to use a commercial product and supplement it with an organic mulch (see "Weeding & Mulching," opposite page), which will break down slowly and filter into the soil.

Choosing & Applying Fertilizer

If the package is emblazoned with the words "citrus food," it's a safe bet the fertilizer inside is appropriate for your citrus trees—but many other products will do just as well. Knowing some basics about fertilizers will help you choose wisely.

By law, the package's front label must display the percentages by weight of nitrogen, phosphorus, and potassium, in that order. A 9-4-8 plant food, for instance, contains 9 percent nitrogen, 4 percent phosphorus (in the form of phosphoric acid), and 8 percent potassium (in the form of potash). Any additional nutrients are itemized in the ingredient list. The remainder of the fertilizer is filler.

Choose a product that is higher in nitrogen than in the other two major nutrients, such as a 14-7-10 formula or the 9-4-8 fertilizer just mentioned. As noted above, a product containing mainly nitrogen does the trick in clay or loam soils, though adding other nutrients doesn't hurt. If you garden in sandy soil, check the label carefully to make sure you're getting the full range of nutrients. In any case, compare the costs of different brands by figuring out how much nitrogen you get for the price. For example, a 5-pound box of 20-

This table will help you figure out roughly how many pounds of fertilizer to apply to get a given amount of nitrogen. For example, to get ¼ pound actual nitrogen from an 10% nitrogen fertilizer, look under 10% and you'll see that you need 2½ pounds of fertilizer.

FERTILIZER/NITROGEN CONVERSION TABLE																	
Actual nitrogen (in lbs.)	Percentages of nitrogen in common fertilizers																
	4%	5	6	7	8	9	10	11	13	15	17	19	21	23	25	29	33
¼	6¼	5	4	3½	3	2¾	2½	2¼	2	1¾	1½	1¼	1¼	1	1	¾	¾
½	12½	10	8¼	7	6¼	5½	5	4½	3¾	3¼	3	2¾	2½	2¼	2	1¾	1½
¾	18¾	15	12½	10¾	9¼	8¼	7½	6¾	5¾	5	4½	4	3¾	3¼	3	2½	2¼
1	25	20	16¾	14¼	12½	11	10	9	7¾	6¾	6	5¼	4¾	4½	4	3½	3

10-10 fertilizer contains twice as much nitrogen as 5 pounds of a 10-8-7 product—so the value is equivalent only if the box containing half the nitrogen costs half as much.

To figure out how much fertilizer to add, you need consider only the product's nitrogen content (if the fertilizer contains a full range of nutrients, your tree will get everything else it needs too). As a rule of thumb, give new citrus trees 2 ounces of actual nitrogen the first year (but only after the tree puts on new growth), then increase by 4 ounces each year for the next few years. After about the fifth year, the tree needs 1 to 1½ pounds of actual nitrogen annually (use the upper end of this range in rainy-summer regions).

To determine the quantity of actual nitrogen in a package of fertilizer, multiply the weight of the fertilizer by the percentage of total nitrogen stated on the label. Or use the chart on the opposite page.

The total amount of fertilizer applied is more important than the precise number or timing of applications. Still, there are a few guidelines. First, take into account the form of plant food you're using. Is it dry or liquid? The most common choice for citrus is dry fertilizer that can be scattered over the root zone and watered in, but liquid plant foods are also sold. (Foliar sprays are applied chiefly to correct nutrient deficiencies; see pages 58–59.) Second, if the fertilizer is dry (granules, stakes, tablets, pellets, powders), is it water-soluble or slow-release? Water-soluble types have a short-lived effect and must be reapplied frequently; plan on at least three (or preferably, four or five) feedings throughout the growing season. Slow-release types, on the other hand, can be applied all at once and possibly just once per year, since they break down gradually, dispensing nutrients over many months.

Climate also plays a role in the timing and frequency of application. In rainy regions, where nutrients wash out of the soil quickly, schedule smaller, more frequent feedings. And if you live in a freeze-prone area, start fertilizing only after the last spring frost and stop in late summer.

WEEDING & MULCHING

A citrus tree is more productive if it doesn't have to compete with weeds for its water and nutrients. Once pesky plants appear, hand-pulling is the preferred way to eliminate them, since hoes and other cultivating tools can damage the tree's surface roots. Better yet, prevent the problem before it begins by spreading a thick layer of mulch over the soil; this will keep many weeds from sprouting. During hot weather, mulch serves another important function: it helps to cool shallow citrus roots and conserve soil moisture. When freezes are expected, though, remove the mulch if it's practical to do so, since bare soil absorbs more warmth than most garden mulches.

Various organic and inorganic materials make suitable mulches. Among the many organic types are homemade compost, wood chips, and leaf mold; inorganic mulches include stone chips and gravel. Organic types eventually break down and work their way into the soil, providing nutrients as they decompose. One caution: if you use woody material, be sure to age it before applying it. The organisms that break down fresh wood chips, sawdust, and so forth need nitrogen to do the job, and they'll take it from the soil—thus depriving your trees.

Take care not to mound organic material against the tree trunk. Keep the mulch about a foot away from the bark to discourage rot diseases and to avoid providing convenient camouflage for rodents and other bark-gnawing pests.

PRUNING

Unlike apples, plums, and other deciduous fruit trees, which are pruned routinely each year, citrus should be pruned only when necessary. Annual pruning diminishes the food reserves of evergreen plants like citrus; and because citrus trees bloom and fruit on new growth, lopping off branch tips reduces the harvest.

In commercial orchards, citrus plants are grown as big shrubs with branches starting low to the ground. If you garden in an intensely sunny climate, you may want to follow this approach to protect the trunk from sunburn. Keeping the bottom branches also gives you a bigger harvest. In humid regions, however, lifting the skirt (removing the lower branches) is advisable as a disease deterrent: the increased open space improves air circulation and minimizes the splashing of fungus spores from soil to tree.

You don't need a lot of fancy pruning equipment to take care of citrus trees. If you attend to unwanted young growth immediately, you can use your fingers to rub or snap it off. Hand pruners efficiently remove tough small-diameter stems; a small pruning saw deals with larger wood.

In freeze-prone areas, avoid pruning in fall or winter: the new growth stimulated by the cuts is especially vulnerable to cold damage.

Reasons to Prune

Though citrus needs little trimming compared to most other fruit trees, you'll sometimes need or want to prune. Here are a few typical pruning jobs.

A citrus tree can be grown with its branches reaching down to the ground or with the lower limbs removed. The 'Valencia' orange trees below illustrate the two options.

Young, tender watersprouts can be snapped off with fingers. Older growth requires pruning shears.

■ Snip off suckers (rootstock growth emerging below the bud union on the trunk or from underground) before they have a chance to overwhelm the upper part of the tree. The rootstock is not the same plant as the scion, so it won't bear the same desirable fruit.

■ Gct rid of watersprouts—vigorous upright shoots growing in undesirable places. They appear on branches, in branch crotches, and along the trunk above the bud union.

■ Remove any growth that makes the tree lopsided.

■ Prune away dead or broken branches. Note, however, that freeze-killed growth should not be removed immediately; see the discussion of cold damage on page 58.

■ Restrain the few vigorous types of citrus, such as true lemons.

■ Rejuvenate a tree by removing dead wood and twiggy, unproductive stems; this allows more light and air through the branches and forces healthy new growth.

■ Remove thc upper limbs of a tree that has grown too tall to suit you.

■ On alternate-bearing trees (mainly certain mandarin varieties that produce a big crop one year and a light one the next), remove some of the fruitlets during a heavy crop year.

■ Train a citrus tree into a pattern; see "Citrus Espaliers" (pages 26–27).

HARVESTING

Some types of fruit continue to mature after being picked, but citrus ripens only on the tree. Judging ripeness can be a bit tricky, though. You can't always rely on rind color: oranges, for example, need cool nights to develop their characteristic hue, so if temperatures remain high, the fruit can be perfectly

At top, a tree-size rootstock sucker with a forked trunk threatens to overwhelm the desirable variety growing from the main trunk at the right. Fell the sucker with a horizontal cut made with a pruning saw (bottom left). A diagonal slice eliminates the stub (bottom right).

Harvest oranges by twisting the fruit as you pull; or clip the stem with hand pruners, as shown here.

CARING FOR CONTAINER CITRUS

Wherever they spend their time—outdoors all year, indoors only during winter, or indoors the year around—potted citrus trees need essentially the same care as citrus in the ground. However, be prepared to water more often, since potted plants, especially those in porous containers such as clay pots, dry out faster than plants with unfettered roots. And don't forget to fertilize: a container-grown tree relies more heavily on you for nutrients than does the same tree in the ground.

Outdoor Care

During dry spells, plan on watering a potted tree as often as every day during warm or windy weather, and about once a week in winter. If you're in doubt about the need for moisture, test the soil with your fingers and water whenever it feels dry beneath the surface. Check in this way even after a rain, since the leaves may have shed most of the water before it reached the soil.

When irrigating by hand, pour water over the entire soil surface, continuing until water flows out the drainage holes. Don't let the plant sit in a saucer full of water, though—if you do, the roots may become soggy. An automated drip system will ease your watering chores. Minisprayers are a good choice for large containers, since they distribute water over the entire root zone; regular drip emitters, in contrast, often cut channels through the soil, bypassing much of the root system.

Since container plants are watered so often, most fertilizers wash out quickly. Save yourself the trouble of constantly replenishing nutrients by using a slow-release product.

Potted citrus can stay outdoors all year in mild-winter climates. However, be ready to move the tree to shelter if a freeze is predicted.

ripe while still green in color. Lemons and limes are ripe when juicy, regardless of whether their peel is green or yellow. The best way to tell if citrus is ripe is simply to pick a fruit and sample it.

The fruit holds best on the tree and should be picked as you need it. Of course, if a hard freeze is predicted, harvest the entire crop and put it in cool storage.

The length of the harvest period depends on the citrus variety and your climate. Kumquats and sour oranges are among the longest-lasting on the tree, hanging on for up to a year without losing their flavor. Most sweet oranges hold for several months, while mandarins—especially satsumas—tend to deteriorate much more quickly. Any variety holds longer in cool climates than in warm regions, especially where nighttime temperatures remain high.

Harvest most citrus by giving it a quick twist as you pull; or remove it by clipping the stem with hand pruners. Loose-skinned mandarins should be harvested only by clipping, since pulling on the fruit carries the risk of tearing off the rind around the stem.

Indoor Care

Citrus trees grown as houseplants need bright light. Set the tree as close as possible to a sunny window (never more than 6 feet away), making sure it's not too close to radiators or other heat sources. If it gets leggy, move it to better light and cut the top back by a third to encourage bushy growth.

If the tree is just wintering indoors, prepare it for the move by gradually reducing the light it receives outdoors. If you shift it abruptly from bright sunshine to relatively low light, you can expect an avalanche of leaves and fruit. When returning the tree outdoors in spring, follow the same plan, giving it increasingly brighter light.

The ideal humidity level for indoor citrus is about 50 percent. If the air isn't moist enough, leaves may drop and branches die back. Heating systems often produce overly dry air, so you'll need to compensate. A humidifier is helpful, but you should also mist the plant and ring it with pebble-filled trays of water (as the water evaporates, it will raise the humidity). If these measures don't solve the problem, move the tree to an unheated room to force it into dormancy.

Keep indoor citrus trees well irrigated while they are actively growing, but water sparingly during winter in cold regions. Apply a slow-release fertilizer that won't wash out with each watering.

Repotting a Container Plant

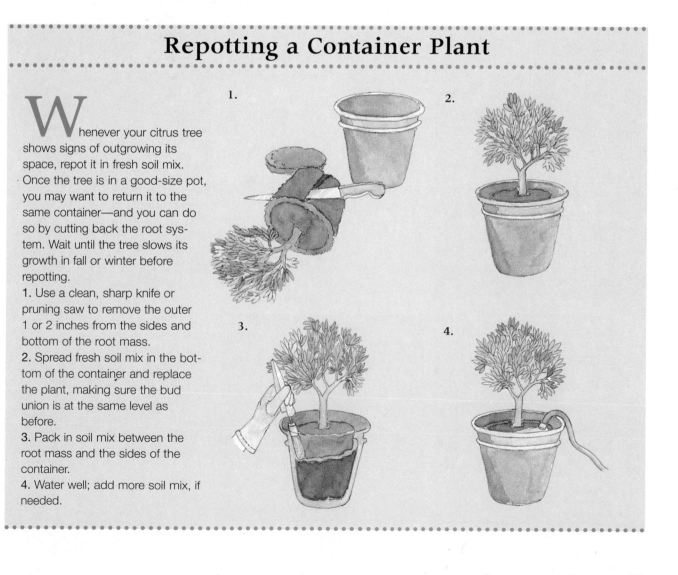

Whenever your citrus tree shows signs of outgrowing its space, repot it in fresh soil mix. Once the tree is in a good-size pot, you may want to return it to the same container—and you can do so by cutting back the root system. Wait until the tree slows its growth in fall or winter before repotting.

1. Use a clean, sharp knife or pruning saw to remove the outer 1 or 2 inches from the sides and bottom of the root mass.

2. Spread fresh soil mix in the bottom of the container and replace the plant, making sure the bud union is at the same level as before.

3. Pack in soil mix between the root mass and the sides of the container.

4. Water well; add more soil mix, if needed.

SOLVING PROBLEMS

By and large, citrus trees flourish in home gardens without having to be mollycoddled or put on a pesticide diet. If you choose suitable varieties, plant properly, and provide sufficient water and nutrients, chances are citrus will succeed for you. That's not to say you won't encounter occasional problems, but most are minor and can either be ignored or resolved by a change in growing conditions. Even damage to the fruit is usually cosmetic, with no effect on eating quality.

Well-maintained citrus trees
rarely develop serious problems.

A Sensible Approach

Pest control is a big part of growing fruit trees such as apples and peaches, but the same doesn't hold true for citrus. Well-tended citrus trees typically have few problems serious enough to require a remedy.

You can spend lots of time fighting small annoyances such as the odd chewed leaf or rind blemish, but learning to accept minor damage is far more sensible. Save your energy to attack problems that actually threaten the health of your trees—after, of course, you've identified the trouble and made sure it warrants action. This chapter describes the most common ailments of citrus; other sources of help include your Cooperative Extension office, the County Agricultural Commissioner's office, and reputable local nurseries.

When you do take action, start with remedies that pose the least danger to people and the environment. Use physical controls whenever practical—for example, blast aphids from their roosts with hard streams of water, or clear away diseased fallen leaves.

When you use biological controls, you defeat a pest with the help of its natural enemies. Many beneficial creatures occur naturally in gardens; others can be purchased, and still others are released as part of biocontrol programs in your state. If you are trying to encourage these helpers, be sure to limit your use of the pesticides that can kill them.

Chemicals are the remedy of last resort. Most citrus problems can be treated with soaps, oils, and copper fungicides; there's seldom a need to use more toxic pesticides, and certainly no need to spray them routinely on your garden. That only kills pests' natural enemies and breeds resistance in the pests themselves, not to mention possibly contaminating the fruit.

Insects & Related Pests

Most citrus pests have numerous natural enemies that keep them in check. If damage occurs, it may be so slight that you can overlook it. If action is required, it usually isn't too drastic: you can vanquish many pests by dislodging them with strong jets of water or by using soap or oil sprays.

Ants

Southern fire ants feed on tender new shoots and bark, sometimes girdling young trees. Other ants inflict indirect harm by driving away natural enemies of sucking pests such as aphids, mealybugs, many types of scale insects, and whiteflies. Such pests excrete a sticky, sugary material called honeydew, on which the ants feed; a column of ants marching up and down the tree trunk usually indicates an infestation by sap feeders.

Control: Place a sticky band on the trunk (prune the canopy up so the ants can't get into the tree without climbing the trunk), or use soap sprays or ant baits.

Aphids

These tiny, pear-shaped, green to black, usually wingless insects come in various types. All suck sap from tender new growth. As the leaves enlarge, they become distorted and curled; blossoms may also be deformed. Heavy feeding can slow the growth of young trees. Aphids excrete honeydew, which attracts ants and promotes the growth of a black mold (sooty mold) on the foliage.

Control: Aim strong jets of water at the pests, or apply soap or oil sprays.

Citrus Leaf Miner

Female moths lay eggs in new leaves, just beneath the surface; when the larvae hatch, they tunnel

Ants

Aphids

Citrus leaf miner

 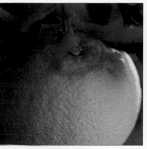   

Citrus nematode   Citrus thrips   Mealybugs   Citrus rust mite   Orangedog caterpillar

through the leaves, creating a winding, blotchy trail. As well as distorting the foliage, heavy infestations can cause defoliation and retard the growth of young trees. This pest is a problem in Florida and Texas.

Control: Apply oil sprays. Commercial orchards have begun releases of a natural enemy.

Citrus Nematode

This microscopic, wormlike pest is found only where citrus has been grown before—in housing developments built on old citrus groves, for example. It feeds on citrus roots, thereby reducing the size of individual fruit and decreasing the total harvest. Serious infestations may result in smaller, yellowed leaves, twig dieback, and a general loss of vigor.

Control: If the pest is present (this must be confirmed by a soil-testing laboratory), there's not much to do but plant new trees with resistant rootstocks. Ask your Cooperative Extension office or County Agricultural Commissioner's office for recommendations.

Citrus Thrips

Barely visible to the naked eye, this slender, orange-yellow insect feeds on tender new leaves and developing fruit. As the leaves expand, they become silvery gray and distorted; the fruit has hard, silvery scars, especially in a ring at the stem end. Found mainly in dry-summer climates, citrus thrips is the biggest pest of citrus in Arizona—but even there, the damage it does is only cosmetic.

Control: None is usually needed. Water adequately, since the insect favors dry plants.

Mealybugs

These insects cluster in cottony masses to suck sap from tender plant tissues. They don't generally inflict serious harm, though their honeydew draws ants and encourages the growth of sooty mold.

Control: Mealybug infestations are usually curbed by natural enemies, so give these helpers a chance by keeping ants away. You can handpick the cottony masses, hose them off with water, or apply soap or oil sprays.

Mites

Various types of these tiny spider relatives are significant citrus pests in all regions. Some feed on leaves, causing yellowing and, in extreme cases, defoliation. Others attack the fruit, scarring or distorting it.

Among the most damaging species is the rind-scarring citrus rust mite; it's the main citrus pest in Florida and Texas and an occasional problem in coastal California. The citrus bud mite is responsible for weirdly deformed fruit, especially on lemons grown on the California coast.

Most mites are so small you need a hand lens to see them. Or check for their presence by holding a sheet of white paper under the affected growth; then tap the plant and look for tiny red, yellow, or green specks crawling on the paper.

Control: Oil sprays are the easiest way to get rid of mites. Lack of water can aggravate some mite problems, so keep trees irrigated.

Orangeworms

This term refers to the various moths and butterflies, such as the orangedog, that chew on citrus leaves, blossoms, or fruit during the caterpillar stage. Severe infestations can ruin fruit or defoliate young trees.

Control: Orangeworms are vulnerable to many natural enemies. If you see only a few caterpillars, handpick them. For larger numbers, spray with the biological insecticide *Bacillus thuringiensis (Bt)*; keep in mind that this control is effective only against young caterpillars when they are feeding. If you're battling a species that rolls itself in leaves, spray before the pests take refuge.

Soaps & Oils

These nonpolluting, nonpersistent pesticides are effective against many harmful organisms. For best results, make sure the tree is well watered, test a small area before covering the whole plant, and avoid spraying in very hot weather (above 90°F/32°C) or in windy conditions.

Soaps

Insecticidal soaps kill soft-bodied insects and mites on contact by penetrating their cell membranes. They're ineffective against pests with tough body coverings and against fast-moving creatures that can evade the spray.

Commercial products are formulated to eliminate pests with minimum harm to plants. Homemade sprays may not be quite so consistently kind to plants, but they're easy to prepare: just mix 2 tablespoons of liquid dishwashing soap with each gallon of water. To slow down drying, apply soap sprays in early morning or late afternoon.

Oils

Horticultural oils kill soft-bodied pests and certain hard-bodied types such as scale insects by smothering them; they're also effective against some fungal diseases. The original kinds were applied to deciduous plants during the dormant season, but summer oils that can be sprayed on leaves are now available.

Though dormant oils may list application rates for use during the growing season, they aren't the same as true summer oils. Summer oils are distilled at a lower temperature, meaning they evaporate faster and are less likely to harm plants. To make sure you're buying a summer oil, look for the words "supreme," "superior," or "narrow-range" on the label.

Avoid spraying in foggy or extremely humid weather; under these conditions, the oil dissipates so slowly it can injure the tree.

Scale Insects

Many species of these pests attack citrus. Immature scales are called crawlers; they first move around the plant, then settle down in colonies to feed on leaves, twigs, or fruit. With maturity, they become immobile and develop a tough coat; at this point, they look less like insects than they do tiny bumps on the plant.

As they suck sap from plant tissues, scales can cause distorted foliage, leaf and fruit drop, and twig dieback; severe infestations can kill young trees. Some types of these pests excrete honeydew, which attracts ants and leads to sooty mold.

Control: Scales have many natural enemies, so give beneficial creatures a helping hand by keeping ants away. Oil sprays are most effective on the crawler stage. For truly serious infestations, a more toxic pesticide mixed with the oil may be in order; ask your Cooperative Extension office or a good nursery for advice. You can pry adults off fruit and scrub them off woody surfaces with a plastic scouring pad.

California red scale

Snails

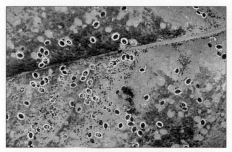
Immature whiteflies

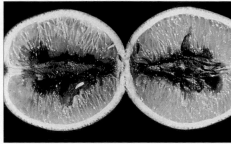
Alternaria black rot

Citrus scab

Slugs & Snails

Snails have a shell and slugs don't, but both these mollusks thrive in shady, moist surroundings. They rasp ragged holes in leaves and fruit at night and on overcast days, taking refuge when the sun is shining. The slimy mucus on which they glide leaves telltale silvery trails.

Control: Mollusks won't cross copper barriers, so you can thwart them by ringing the tree trunk with copper (prune the canopy up so the pests can't bypass the barrier). Other measures include handpicking, baits, traps, and decollate snails. (In California, the release of these predatory snails is legal only in the nine Southern California counties.)

Whiteflies

Various types of whiteflies, including the citrus blackfly, suck sap from leaf undersides, sometimes turning the foliage yellow. The immature insects look like little transparent spots. The adults resemble tiny white moths (or black ones, in the case of the citrus blackfly). The pests excrete honeydew, which attracts ants and promotes the growth of sooty mold.

Control: Whiteflies have many natural enemies, so it's important to keep ants away and to forgo sprays that could kill beneficial creatures. In Florida, a fungal disease sometimes attacks immature whiteflies, turning them white, red, or yellow; if you see such afflicted pests, leave them to their doom.

WILDLIFE

Young trees are most prone to injury from wildlife; for example, rabbits can kill a tree by stripping the bark. To deter animals that can be fenced out, start trees in wire cages. Once the plants reach a good size, they can tolerate some damage; periodic incursions from birds pecking holes in fruit or deer browsing on leaves won't be as noticeable.

Burrowing animals such as pocket gophers, ground squirrels, and armadillos can be a real nuisance, though they don't single out citrus as a special target for destruction. Some pesky rodents can be controlled by trapping or poison, but other bothersome animals may be protected by law, so inquire with your state's Game or Conservation Department before you get out the heavy artillery.

DISEASES

Though citrus is vulnerable to assorted fungi and viruses, it fares pretty well in home gardens. To dodge trouble, start off with healthy trees from a reputable source; if a particular disease is rampant in your
area, ask about resistant varieties. When you plant, choose a location with good drainage. Keep in mind that, despite all precautions, it's hard to avoid some damage from fungal diseases in wet climates, where rain splashes spores around.

Alternaria Diseases

This fungus may infect susceptible varieties during rainy weather. In spring, it produces brown spots on the leaves and rind of 'Minneola' and 'Orlando' tangelo, 'Murcott' tangor, and 'Dancy' mandarin. Infected leaves drop, but fruit damage is usually superficial.

In late summer or early fall, the fungus causes black rot mainly in navel oranges. The rot starts at the stem and extends into the core; then the fruit drops.

Control: Copper fungicides can prevent infection if applied early enough.

Citrus Scab

A fungal disease, citrus scab is a problem primarily in Florida, affecting mainly 'Temple' and 'Murcott' tangor, satsuma mandarin, sour orange, and lemon. It may occasionally strike grapefruit. Scablike, corky brown areas develop on the rind, leaves, and twigs. In early spring, spores released from old lesions infect new growth.

No Problem

You may think your citrus tree has a condition that needs curing when nothing is really wrong. Here are some examples.

Alternate Bearing

The tendency to produce a large crop one year and a light harvest the next affects mainly 'Valencia' orange (though not as much in Florida as in other regions) and many mandarins. To balance the yields, remove some of the fruit (when it's still tiny and green) during a heavy-bearing year.

Flower & Fruit Drop

Citrus trees produce far more flowers and fruit than they can possibly support, so they self-thin: less than 5 percent of the blossoms produce mature fruit. The majority of the flowers drop during and right after bloom. A heavy shedding of immature fruit takes place afterward; another fruit drop occurs when the remaining fruitlets are very small. Once the fruit reaches about an inch in diameter, it generally stays on the tree.

Fruit Splitting

Citrus fruit, especially navel oranges, may crack and split in autumn. The usual cause is a late growth spurt brought on by rain and cooling temperatures; the skin of the fruit can't expand fast enough to keep up with the flesh.

Irregular or excessive watering can aggravate the problem. Splitting ordinarily affects only a few fruits on the tree.

Inferior Fruit

Many types of citrus, especially satsuma mandarins, produce thick-skinned, bland-tasting fruit for the first few years after planting—but the quality usually improves markedly as the tree matures.

Citrus trees that normally set fruit once a year—during the spring growth flush—may produce at other times. This off-bloom fruit, especially that of sweet orange, grapefruit, and tangelo, is thick-skinned, puffy, and sheep-nosed (slightly pointy at one end). Good growing practices, including consistent watering, will minimize the problem.

If the poor-quality fruit doesn't even resemble the type produced by the citrus variety you're growing, it may be rootstock fruit. Look to see if the growth bearing this fruit has come from below the bud union. If so, prune it off at the trunk before it overwhelms the scion.

Regreening

Ripe fruit remaining on the tree during hot weather may revert from orange to green. This phenomenon is most often observed in 'Valencia' orange. The flavor of the fruit is unaffected.

Sports

These genetic mutations, also called chimeras, involve only part of the tree. Most common in navel orange and grapefruit, sports have leaves or fruit different in color or shape from those on the rest of the tree: for example, the foliage on the affected branch may be variegated or the fruit distorted. Sports are typically inferior, but every now and then, one leads to an improved variety.

Fruit splitting

Regreening

Sports

| Greasy spot | Melanose | Brown rot | Foot rot | Root rot | Sooty mold |

Control: Damage doesn't usually warrant action. If you spray a copper fungicide, do so once as new growth emerges, then again during petal fall. Destroy diseased leaves and fruit.

Greasy Spot

Found in hot, humid climates, this fungal disease causes rind blemishes and premature leaf drop in all types of citrus, especially grapefruit. Marred fruit is edible, but damage to the foliage can cause defoliation. The leaf undersides show yellowish spots that turn dark, resembling blotches of grease; heavily infected leaves will drop.

Control: Spray oil or a copper fungicide, or both, in early summer. Get rid of fallen leaves, since the fungus survives on them.

Melanose

Another fungal disease of hot, humid regions, melanose strikes mainly grapefruit. The first signs of infection are tiny light brown spots on rind, leaves, and twigs. These spots darken and become sandpapery, then spread to form large scars. On fruit, they often appear in rings or tear-streak patterns, since the spores are washed over the surface by rain.

Control: There's no need to spray, since the damage to fruit is cosmetic. If you apply a copper

fungicide, do so once at petal fall, then again as the fruit develops. Also remove dead wood, since the fungus spends part of its life there.

Phytophthora Diseases

Several species of this soil-borne fungus cause problems in all regions. The name of the disease varies, depending on which part of the tree is infected.

Brown Rot   Brown rot occurs when *Phytophthora* infects the fruit. The spores are splashed from the soil onto the lower part of the tree by rain or irrigation water, causing brown spots on the rind. In Florida, the rot can get into the flesh; in other regions, damage is usually superficial. Infected fruit may spoil in storage after harvest.

Control: Prune off branches that touch the ground; keep weeds under control to improve air circulation and to minimize splashing of spores onto the tree.

Foot Rot or Gummosis   This malady results when *Phytophthora* infects the tree trunk. Sap oozes from cracks; the inner bark is brown and gummy, but the discoloration doesn't go all the way into the wood. A badly infected tree loses vigor and will die if the rot girdles the trunk, cutting off the flow of water and nutrients.

In Texas and Florida, where the prevalent rootstocks are resistant to

Phytophthora, the infection is usually found just above the bud union and is called foot rot. In the West, the disease is known as gummosis when it appears higher up on the trunk; if it spreads down into the crown (where the trunk and roots meet), it's sometimes called foot rot.

Control: Plant trees at the proper depth and keep mounded soil and water away from the trunk. Improve ventilation by removing branches touching the ground and eliminating weeds. Avoid injuring the bark with a lawnmower or pruning tools, since wounds give the fungus an entry point. In some areas, systemic fungicides may be available to treat the disease.

Root Rot   When *Phytophthora* attacks the root system—an occurrence most common in heavy, poorly drained soils—the resulting disease is called root rot. The feeder roots are destroyed, limiting the uptake of water and nutrients. The top of the tree declines slowly; the leaves turn yellow and may drop.

Control: Don't plant citrus where it will be irrigated along with the lawn or other plants that are watered frequently.

Sooty Mold

This fungus, most active in cool, moist conditions, feeds on honeydew, the plant sap excreted by aphids, mealybugs, many types of scale insects, and whiteflies. A black film forms on the surface of the leaves, making them appear sooty.

Control: Hose off the tree; keep sap feeders in check.

Stubborn Disease

This incurable viruslike disease affects primarily sweet orange, grapefruit, and tangelo trees grown in hot inland areas of California and in the desert. Telltale signs include small, lopsided fruit, stunted growth, and small leaves held upright instead of flat; afflicted trees may produce inferior off-bloom fruit.

Control: None. If a young tree is infected, it will remain small and produce meager harvests. On a mature tree, only one or two branches may be affected, and the disease may or may not spread.

Tristeza Virus

This virus can be fatal to citrus. Though it can be transmitted by some types of aphids, it is usually spread by importing infected plants into an area or by using infected budwood. For this reason, all citrus-growing states have instituted programs to restrict the movement of citrus plants and to provide propagators with healthy wood.

Tristeza virus is widespread in Florida and Southern California.

Afflicted trees do not always die; they may simply stop growing and producing fruit for a few years, then just as suddenly partially recover.

Sour orange and *Citrus macrophylla* rootstocks are especially susceptible. The disease is present in many old 'Meyer' lemon trees— hence the replacement of that variety by 'Improved Meyer'.

Control: None. Use resistant or tolerant rootstocks when planting new trees.

ENVIRONMENTAL DISORDERS

Some problems are due to unfavorable growing conditions rather than pests or diseases.

Cold Damage

Leaves and twigs appear water-soaked, then wither and darken. The leaves may drop quickly or persist on the tree for weeks. When the fruit freezes, the affected areas of the flesh dry out and brownish pits called ice marks may form on the rind above them. On a severely cold-damaged tree, branches die back and the bark may split.

Though your impulse may be to remove frost-killed wood at once, hold off and give the tree a chance to recover. After new growth

appears in late winter or early spring, wait for any dieback. Then cut back to live wood (identifiable by a green layer just under the bark). The pruning cuts will heal naturally, so there's no need to paint them with any compound.

Excessive Fruit Drop

If your citrus tree sheds most or all of its fruit, the cause may be a sudden change in temperature, especially a heat wave at fruit set or shortly thereafter. Other factors triggering fruit drop include too much or too little moisture, lack of nutrients, and damage from pesticide sprays. The problem is most common in young trees.

Nutrient Deficiencies

When citrus trees don't get the nutrients they need, they show characteristic symptoms of the shortage. You can often identify the deficiency by paying attention to the pattern of leaf yellowing (chlorosis) and noting whether it occurs in new or old foliage.

Solving deficiencies is usually a matter of adding the relevant nutrient. When plants are lacking in zinc, iron, or manganese, the problem may not be that the nutrient is actually missing, but that it is present in a form unavailable to plant roots. In these cases, it's important

Stubborn disease

Tristeza virus

Nitrogen deficiency

to apply the mineral to the soil in chelated form (which roots can extract) or to spray it on the leaves.

The following are the most common deficiencies affecting citrus trees.

Nitrogen   Since nitrogen is in short supply in all soils and plants need large amounts of it, this is the deficiency you'll encounter most often. Starting with the older leaves near the bottom of the tree, the foliage turns a uniform yellow, then drops. In severe cases, growth is stunted and the tree may bloom profusely but not set much fruit. To make up for the deficiency, apply a high-nitrogen fertilizer.

Zinc   Young leaves are abnormally small, with yellow blotches between the veins. The symptoms are usually more obvious on the south side of the tree. Zinc deficiency is common in alkaline soils; to cure it, treat affected trees with a foliar spray.

Iron   Young leaves gradually turn yellow between the veins. The veins themselves remain green, though in severe cases, they too lose color. Only part of the citrus tree may be affected.

Iron deficiency is common in soils that are alkaline, poorly drained, or overwatered. Correcting these conditions often clears up the problem, but if it does not, add chelated iron; sprays are ineffective.

Manganese   Young leaves turn a lighter green between the veins. In severe cases, the interveinal color fades to nearly white and the affected leaves drop. Symptoms are usually more noticeable on the north side of the tree.

Manganese deficiency may occur along with a deficiency of zinc or iron (or both). It often disappears as leaves mature, but if it persists, apply a foliar spray.

Magnesium   Older leaves turn yellow between the veins and may drop. Symptoms are most apparent in late summer or fall.

This deficiency is common in rainy climates, since magnesium is easily leached from the soil. Apply a foliar spray or add magnesium sulfate or dolomitic lime to the soil.

Sunburn

Citrus bark is prone to damage in hot-sun areas, especially in desert regions. The sunburned wood becomes brittle and may peel off in patches. Heavily pruned and young trees are most vulnerable to injury.

A simple solution is to wrap the trunk in white cardboard or in the paper trunk bands available from commercial suppliers. An alternative is to apply whitewash or flat latex paint, either in white or in a light brown shade that blends with the trunk color. If heavy pruning has exposed any limbs, paint those too.

Another way to protect the trunk is to let the branches grow to the ground, though that complicates harvesting. Some gardeners cut an opening into the skirt so they can get to fruit inside the tree.

Citrus fruit can also sunburn. The rind develops tough, brownish spots where it's exposed to hot sun, and the flesh may dry out.

Wind Injury

Strong winds can damage fruit and leaves or knock them right off the tree. Twigs rubbing against the rind will scar the fruit; these blemishes are sometimes confused with citrus thrips damage, but they're random and don't appear in a ring around the stem end.

Hot, drying winds can cause bronzing, pitting, and curling of foliage, primarily on the outside of the canopy facing the wind. Cold winds from the ocean can stunt trees.

In windy areas, plant citrus in a sheltered spot or install a windbreak; either a row of tall trees or a structure is effective.

Zinc deficiency

Iron deficiency

Manganese deficiency

Magnesium deficiency

Symptoms & Possible Causes

In the following list, we note some common ailments of citrus and suggest possible causes. If you can't determine the specific source of a problem with the help of this chapter, consult your Cooperative Extension office, County Agricultural Commissioner's office, or a reputable local nursery.

Symptom	Possible Causes	Notes
Yellow leaves	Nitrogen deficiency	Uniform yellowing; see page 59.
	Overwatering	
	Mites	See page 53.
	Whiteflies	See page 55.
	Root damage	Citrus nematode (page 53), burrowing wildlife (page 55), root rot (page 57).
	Greasy spot	See page 57.
Mottled leaves	Natural on some varieties	Genetic variegation.
	Sport	Affects only part of tree; see page 56.
	Nutrient deficiencies	See pages 58–59.
	Citrus leaf miner	See page 52.
Distorted leaves	Insect pests	Aphids (page 52), citrus leaf miner (page 52), citrus thrips (page 53), scale insects (page 54).
	Citrus scab	See page 55.
Leaf drop	Normal shedding of old leaves	Mainly during spring bloom.
	Too much or too little water	
	High temperatures	
	Low humidity	
	Nutrient deficiencies	See pages 58–59.
	Wind injury	See page 59.
	Pests	Mites (page 53), citrus leaf miner (page 52), scale insects (page 54).
	Fungus diseases	*Alternaria* brown spot (page 55), greasy spot (page 57), root rot (page 57).
Misshapen fruit	Citrus bud mite	See page 53.
	Stubborn disease	See page 58.
	Off-bloom fruit	See "Inferior Fruit," page 56.

Symptom	Possible Causes	Notes
Scarred fruit	Citrus thrips	See page 53.
	Mites	See page 53.
	Fungus diseases	Brown rot (page 57), citrus scab (page 55), melanose (page 57).
	Sunburn	See page 59.
	Wind injury	See page 59.
Different fruit than expected	Rootstock has taken over	Growth comes from below bud union; see "Inferior Fruit," page 56.
	Sport	Affects only part of tree; see page 56.
Fruit drop	Normal self-thinning	Until fruit is about an inch in diameter; see "Flower & Fruit Drop," page 56.
	Sudden temperature changes	
	Too much or too little water	
	Nutrient deficiencies	See pages 58–59.
	Wind injury	See page 59.
	Scale insects	See page 54.
	Alternaria black rot	See page 55.
Small crop	Alternate bearing	See page 56.
	Excessive fruit drop	See page 58.
	Very young tree	Size of crop increases as tree matures.
Stunted growth	Nitrogen deficiency	See page 59.
	Root damage	Citrus nematode (page 53), burrowing wildlife (page 55), root rot (page 57).
	Diseases	Stubborn disease (page 58), tristeza virus (page 58).
	Scale insects	See page 54.
	Persistent cold winds	
Dieback	Cold damage	See page 58.
	Scale insects	See page 54.
	Citrus nematode	See page 53.
Trunk wound	Foot rot or gummosis	Oozing sap and brown, gummy inner bark; see page 57.
	Mechanical injury	Inflicted by lawnmower or weed trimmer; no oozing or gumminess unless wound becomes infected.
	Sunburn	Bark peels off in patches; see page 59.

ENCYCLOPEDIA OF CITRUS

What's the "navel" in a navel orange? Why are blood oranges burgundy red? What's a tangor? How did breeders come up with the limequat? What do you do with a citron? The following pages answer these and other questions about citrus. In addition to overviews of the many citrus types, you'll find detailed descriptions of more than 80 different varieties. For an at-a-glance summary of these varieties and where they grow best, consult the chart beginning on page 90.

Seven kinds of citrus trees grow in brick-edged planting beds in this backyard herb garden.

SWEET ORANGE

Who could resist eating sweet oranges or drinking their juice? Certainly not modern-day Americans, who consume huge quantities of oranges every year. Yet only a few centuries ago, Europeans grew oranges primarily as ornamental plants prized for their fragrant flowers and peel.

Brought from China to the Middle East and the Mediterranean region by Arab traders, the sweet orange was first cultivated in Europe in the 15th century. It soon gained elite status: royalty went wild over orange trees, housing them in special glass-walled buildings which came to be called *orangeries*. The

'Cara Cara' navel

fruit became a common motif in Renaissance paintings and was even adopted as a symbol of the de Medici family.

The sweet orange made the sea voyage to the New World. It was planted in Florida in the 16th century, then spread westward with missionaries. And a little more than a century ago, as marketers recognized the potential of selling the delectable fruit on a mass scale, oranges became big business. Today, the sweet orange is more widely grown than any other type of citrus.

Sweet orange trees typically form dense globes to about 25 feet tall. The plants are hardy to around 25°F/−4°C, withstanding a bit more cold than true lemons but not as much as mandarins.

Though these oranges are referred to as "sweet," the term is misleading: the flesh contains a blend of sugar and acid. Since sugar forms during hot days and acid during cool nights, the most flavorful fruit is found in regions with wide daily fluctuations in temperature. The appellation "sweet" also distinguishes these oranges from sour types (see page 69) and from the acidless or sugar oranges popular in other parts of the world.

The many types of sweet oranges ripen at various times

of year and grow in climates ranging from fairly cool to intensely hot. Even in the warmest areas, the fruit usually stores on the tree for a few months.

In the United States, the foremost commercial sweet orange crops are navels for eating fresh and 'Valencia' for juice. Home gardeners have access to these and many other, less well-known varieties; choose according to your climate, the type of orange you want, and the preferred harvest time.

NAVEL ORANGES

This sort of orange has an undeveloped secondary fruit embedded in the end opposite the stem, creating a hole that looks like a navel. Big and seedless, navel oranges are easy to peel and divide into sections. They're superior for eating and can be squeezed—though the juice has a delayed bitterness that limits the amount permitted in commercial orange juice.

Navels have a more restricted range than many other oranges. They're deliciously sweet in the humid subtropics; in the West, they have a richer, more complex flavor. Outstanding crops are produced in inland valleys of California with moderate summer heat and some winter cold. The fruit is somewhat tart when grown near the coast. Navels can succeed in the desert, especially in the Phoenix area—but crops there are a bit small, since hot, dry weather in late spring causes petal drop.

Navel oranges ripen early, allowing harvest before cold can damage the crop. In California, late varieties are available to extend the season.

'Washington'

This is the original navel variety, shipped to the United States from Brazil in 1870. It was named in honor of Washington, D.C., where it was propagated before being sent to sunnier climes for trial planting a few years later.

The trees that took root in Southern California were so perfectly suited to the climate that they spurred the growth of the citrus industry in the Western United States. One of the original trees still stands in Riverside, a living monument to the impact of the navel orange on California—and on the West as a whole.

Excellent flavor has kept 'Washington' popular among commercial growers and home gardeners alike. The oranges ripen from fall into winter and store on the tree for 3 to 4 months.

Sports of 'Washington'

Navel orange trees are sometimes unstable, producing sports—mutations that affect only a branch or two. These mutations occasionally have desirable traits, in which case they may be developed into separate varieties.

All the varieties listed below began their existence as sports of 'Washington'. Selections grown in Florida and Texas often have no variety name and are sold under the generic name "navel."

'Cara Cara'   This is the first pigmented navel variety. Despite the reddish color, it isn't a blood orange with a navel: not only is a different pigment involved, but the flavor is straight navel orange, with no berry overtones.

Found on a 'Washington' tree in Venezuela, 'Cara Cara' was released in Florida, where its flesh is a fairly deep red and the plants are often labeled "red navel." California-grown 'Cara Cara' is pink-fleshed, though the fruit hardly colors up at all near the coast. The crop ripens at about the same time as 'Washington'.

'Fukumoto'   This relatively new variety is noteworthy for its excellent flavor and for an attractive orange-red rind similar to that of 'Minneola' tangelo. It ripens about a week before 'Washington'.

'Lane Late'   Discovered in Australia, this variety ripens 4 to 6 weeks later than 'Washington'. The fruit is similar to that of 'Washington' but has a smaller navel.

Other, newer late-ripeners from Australia making their way to this country include 'Autumn Gold', 'Barnfield', 'Chislett Late', 'Powell Late', and 'Summergold'. Because they are patented varieties, they may be hard to find, since growers are often reluctant to pay fees to propagate them.

'Robertson'   The fruit of 'Robertson' is identical to that of 'Washington', but it ripens 2 to 3 weeks earlier and is usually carried in clusters. Dwarf trees are amazingly prolific.

'Skaggs Bonanza'   This variety ripens about 2 weeks earlier and bears more heavily than 'Washington', but it doesn't hold its fruit as well. The tree is smaller and denser than its parent.

Arizona Sweets

This name refers to the non-navel oranges favored in Arizona because they generally ripen before hard frosts. 'Hamlin', 'Marrs', 'Pineapple', and 'Trovita' are the main varieties. 'Diller', a small, seedy juice variety originating in Arizona, is still grown, but its popularity has declined.

The plant tag may refer only to "Arizona Sweets" without specifying the variety. Ask nursery personnel for help if you're looking for a particular orange.

'Pineapple'

'Spring'   A recently introduced late navel from California, 'Spring' matures at about the same time as 'Lane Late' but has bigger fruit with a deeper orange color.

COMMON ORANGES

This catchall category includes the many non-navel sweet oranges. Late-ripening 'Valencia' predominates, but other, earlier varieties are also available to home gardeners.

'Hamlin'

The most widely grown early orange in Florida, 'Hamlin' is also cultivated in Texas and Arizona. Excellent for juicing, the small, low-acid, nearly seedless fruit ripens from fall into winter.

'Jaffa'

Also called 'Shamouti', this midseason Israeli variety is an attractive plant that thrives wherever navels do. From winter into spring, it produces a heavy crop of large, thick-skinned, nearly seedless oranges that are delicious eaten fresh.

'Marrs'

A navel-less sport of 'Washington', this early orange is grown primarily in Texas (where it was discovered) and Arizona.

The small tree bears from fall into winter, producing a heavy crop of medium-size, low-acid oranges that, though juicy, are best suited for eating fresh. The fruit can become seedy if pollinators are grown nearby.

'Parson Brown'

Until it was supplanted by 'Hamlin' more than 30 years ago, this big, vigorous tree was the main early-season variety in Florida—and it's still best suited to that state. The pale yellow–fleshed, small, seedy oranges are excellent for juicing.

'Pineapple'

The main midseason orange in Florida, 'Pineapple' is also grown in Texas and Arizona— even though it's somewhat cold-sensitive. An alternate bearer, it's especially prone to damage during those winters when it produces heavily. The medium-size, fairly seedy, rich-flavored fruit is popular for juicing. It tends to drop from the tree after maturity.

'Trovita'

This navel-less sport of 'Washington' is more widely adapted than its parent, thriving not only in moderate climates but also in the desert and near the coast. The fruit is even flavorful in sunny parts of the San Francisco Bay Area.

The medium-size oranges contain few seeds; they ripen a little later than 'Washington', from winter into spring. Juicier than a navel, the fruit is fine for eating or juicing. Plants tend to bear heavily every other year.

'Valencia'

Originally from Portugal but named for a region of Spain, 'Valencia' is the most widely grown citrus variety in the world and the premier juice orange.

The big, vigorous plants are more widely adapted than navels, succeeding in climates ranging from very hot to fairly cool. The fruit is medium to large, with few seeds and a slightly more acid flavor than a navel. It ripens as early as midwinter in the warmest regions, but not until the beginning of summer in the coolest parts of its range. 'Valencia' oranges store on the tree for many months, actually improving in flavor as they hang.

In areas of the country where citrus is subject to cold damage, the lateness of the crop can be a problem. Earlier-ripening varieties are a better bet in Arizona, Texas, and chancy areas of Florida.

'Valencia' typically bears heavily in alternate years, though this tendency is less pronounced in Florida than in other regions. Alternate bearing shouldn't bother home gardeners, though, since the fruit holds so long and crops often overlap.

In hot weather, ripe 'Valencia' oranges may "regreen"—revert from orange to green. The color change doesn't affect fruit quality.

Improved 'Valencia' Types

'Valencia' has given rise to some new varieties, though not as many as 'Washington' navel has. Some ('Olinda' and 'Cutter', for example) aren't usually sold under separate names, but the following three types are.

'Delta'   This seedless South African variety ripens 2 to 3 weeks earlier than 'Valencia' and sets more of its fruit inside the canopy, where it's protected from the elements.

'Midknight'   Another seedless variety from South Africa, 'Midknight' matures 2 to 4 weeks before 'Valencia'. The fruit is big, with superior flavor.

'Rohde Red'   This nearly seedless selection boasts deeper orange flesh for more attractive juice. The color difference is evident only in Florida; in California, 'Rohde Red' looks just like plain 'Valencia'.

'Valencia'

Blood Orange

This type of sweet orange is noteworthy both for its reddish or purplish pigmentation and for its rich, berry-tinged flavor. Unfortunately, many people find the name "blood orange" so off-putting that they're reluctant to try the fruit; to solve this problem, some nurserymen have suggested changing the name to "burgundy orange."

Blood oranges are rarely sold in U.S. grocery stores, but they've long been popular for eating, juice, and garnishes in Europe. In fact, the main varieties grown in this country come from Spain and Italy.

The trees, which reach a height of 20 to 25 feet as standards, are ideally suited to areas with wide fluctuations between day and night temperatures: the fruit needs warm days for sugars to form, cool nights for color to develop. The best growing regions are warm inland valleys of California; results are inconsistent in the desert. With the exception of 'Moro', blood oranges are marginal in coastal Northern California. In Florida and Texas, they develop little or no red pigmentation—a fact which may seem surprising, given that these two states are well known for red-fleshed grapefruit. The explanation is simply that blood oranges get their color from anthocyanins, the same pigments that cause many deciduous trees to turn red and purple in autumn; an entirely different pigment makes red grapefruit varieties turn rosy.

Rind color is most intense on fruit shielded from the sun inside the canopy or on the shady side of the tree.

The juicy, medium-size oranges, which contain few to no seeds, begin to ripen in early winter in the warmest areas; on the California coast, ripening does not begin until spring. Blood oranges don't hold on the tree as long as other sweet oranges.

Enjoy these oranges fresh, as fruit or juice. For a delicious, rosy-hued drink with a berry flavor, blend the juice with that of other citrus types.

'Moro'

'Moro'

This variety bears clusters of oranges with a red-blushed rind and sweet-tart, deep burgundy flesh. The fruit is generally round, though the shape can vary, even among oranges on the same tree.

A spreading, vigorous tree, 'Moro' is the only variety to develop good flavor and flesh color in cool coastal Northern California. It usually colors up well in the desert.

'Sanguinelli'

Of the three varieties discussed here, 'Sanguinelli' bears the smallest oranges. The oval fruit has tart-sweet, burgundy-streaked orange flesh that isn't quite as colorful as the highly pigmented rind might lead you to expect. The rosy-skinned fruit makes the plant decorative as a specimen or in a container.

'Tarocco'

Though bearing larger, sweeter oranges than either 'Moro' or 'Sanguinelli', 'Tarocco' has the least reliable pigmentation. The color is best in warm inland valleys.

Open growth and long, willowy, vinelike branches make this variety a good choice for espalier.

Sour orange

'Bouquet de Fleurs'

Originating in Asia, the sour orange (also called bitter orange) spread first to the Middle East and North Africa, then moved on to Europe during the 10th century— beating the sweet orange by several hundred years. So closely associated with Spain were these tart fruits that they became known as Seville oranges. Even after the advent of sweet orange orchards on European soil, the sour type was for a time more widely grown: the blossoms had a more intense fragrance and the fruit made a better seasoning.

The sour orange trees grown in the United States are extremely ornamental, sporting handsome foliage and large, perfumed, waxy white flowers. Clusters of deep red-orange, very juicy, fairly large fruits ripen in mid-fall to late winter and store well on the tree, adorning the branches for nearly a year. The flavor is both sour and bitter—sour due to the fruit's acidic juice, bitter due to essential oils.

Since the fruit doesn't have to sweeten, sour orange does well in cool-summer regions. The trees are quite cold-hardy, almost as much so as kumquats.

Commercially, sour oranges are used in premium marmalades and orange-flavored liqueurs such as Cointreau; they also make good chutney, candied fruit, and pies. In China, both fruit and blossoms are used in tea.

Another important use of the sour orange tree is as a rootstock for other types of citrus.

'Bouquet de Fleurs'

Also sold as 'Bouquet', this variety is considered the most fragrant of all citrus: the plentiful blossoms are so heavily scented that their oils are used in the French perfume industry.

A spreading, thornless plant only 8 to 10 feet tall, 'Bouquet de Fleurs' makes an especially lovely specimen, patio tree, or hedge. Its fruit contains few seeds.

'Chinotto'

Densely clothed with small, myrtlelike foliage (the tree is sometimes sold as myrtle-leaf orange), 'Chinotto' is a thornless variety that grows slowly to 7 feet or a little taller. Compact and rounded, it makes a wonderful foundation plant or hedge and will even grow happily for years in an 8- to 10-inch container. Its fruit is seedy.

'Seville'

This thorny, upright, 20- to 30-foot tree with long, pointed leaves is the traditional ornamental tree of Mediterranean courtyards. Used as a street tree in Arizona and Southern California, it also makes a good specimen, hedge, or tall screen.

'Seville' is still important commercially in Spain, since its seedy fruit makes outstanding marmalade.

MANDARIN

The many mandarin varieties are noted for their loose-skinned fruit— sometimes described as "zipper-skinned," since it peels so easily. An outmoded name is "kid-glove orange": a lady could supposedly strip the rind and eat the easy-to-separate segments without even removing her gloves.

The name "mandarin" is a clue to the fruit's origin: this type of citrus has been cultivated in China for thousands of years. It had already spread throughout Asia by the 10th century, but reached Europe only in the early 1800s. Varieties with a red-orange peel are often called tangerines, a term said to have arisen when an early mandarin was shipped to England from the Moroccan port of Tangier. But in fact all varieties, whether red-tinted or not, are mandarins.

Though they form a large and varied group, mandarins share some traits. Most are small to medium-size trees— from about 10 to 20 feet tall— with fairly small leaves and few or no thorns. The juicy, often flattened fruit is smaller and typically sweeter than a sweet orange. Most varieties mature in winter, though some bear earlier or later.

One problem with many mandarins is a tendency toward alternate bearing— producing a heavy crop one year followed by a light one the next. Removing some of the fruit during heavy crop years helps even things out.

Mandarins tolerate a wide range of growing conditions, and there's a variety for just about every climate in the citrus belt. Most accept heat but don't need much to produce a good crop. In general, the fruit doesn't store on the tree as long as sweet oranges do; harvest it at peak ripeness, before the rind gets puffy or the flesh loses its flavor.

A mandarin's foliage is usually more cold-resistant than that of a sweet orange, but the fruit is not. In borderline areas, minimize damage to the fruit by growing early-ripening varieties.

Though mandarins can be used as a flavoring or in beverages, they're so wonderfully sweet and juicy that most people enjoy eating them fresh.

'CLEMENTINE'

Also called Algerian tangerine, this fairly small, semi-open, spreading tree produces fruit with a red-orange rind and sweet, juicy flesh containing few to many seeds. The fruit ripens from late fall into winter; it holds on the tree longer than that of most other mandarin varieties.

Best suited to hot climates, 'Clementine' can also bear tasty fruit in cooler regions. Fruiting is usually light unless the trees are planted near another mandarin or a tangelo (see page 73) for pollination.

'Clementine' has produced numerous hybrids (see pages 74–75); it also has earlier- and later-ripening selections, which may be sold under separate names.

'Dancy'

'DANCY'

This is the "tangerine" found in supermarkets in the winter holiday season. The red-orange fruit is usually slightly necked at the stem end and is smaller and seedier than most other mandarins. Fruiting is typically heavy in alternate years.

An erect, vigorous tree, 'Dancy' needs high heat to produce sweet, flavorful fruit. It's best suited to its native Florida; good harvests can also be produced in the desert, though exposed fruit is often sunburned.

'ENCORE'

The result of a cross between 'Mediterranean' and the old variety 'King', 'Encore' is so named because it ripens later than most other varieties: the fruit matures from spring into summer and holds on the tree until fall.

The upright, slender-branched tree produces seedy, sweet-tart mandarins with a thin, splotchy yellowish orange rind. It tends to bear heavily every other year.

'FREMONT'

A hybrid between 'Clementine' and 'Ponkan', this alternate bearer produces its crop of bright orange, seedy, very sweet mandarins from late fall and on into winter. The fruit stores fairly well on the tree.

'HONEY'

Like 'Encore', this vigorous tree is a 'Mediterranean' × 'King' hybrid and an alternate bearer. Its small, seedy, very sweet fruit is borne from winter into spring.

A California variety, 'Honey' is quite different from Florida's 'Murcott' tangor (see page 73), which is sold under the name Honey tangerine in markets.

'KARA'

A cross between 'Owari' satsuma and 'King', this alternate bearer doesn't tolerate cold winters or desert heat. Its springtime crop of big, deep orange, sweet-tart fruit may be very seedy one year, nearly seedless the next. The fruit should be harvested soon after reaching maturity, since the rind quickly becomes puffy.

'Kara' has the best flavor when grown in the warm interior climates of California; fruit produced near the coast is a bit tart, though it's still tasty.

'KINNOW'

Columnar, densely foliaged 'Kinnow' does well in all the West's citrus climates. Like other hybrids derived from 'Mediterranean' and 'King', it's an alternate bearer.

The fruit begins ripening in winter in the warmest

areas. Yellow-orange and seedy, it's hard to peel and too sweet for many palates. It holds fairly well on the tree.

'MEDITERRANEAN'

Also called 'Willow Leaf' for its willowlike growth, this variety was the first mandarin to be grown in the Mediterranean basin. Its tendency for alternate bearing has been passed on to the many hybrids developed from it. The sweet, aromatic, yelloworange, very juicy fruit matures in winter to spring; the rind gets puffy soon after ripening. High heat is essential for a tasty crop.

'PIXIE'

A late-maturing variety best suited to coastal and inland California, 'Pixie' produces

'Pixie'

yellowish orange, seedless fruit with a mild, sweet flavor. It ripens in early spring and holds until summer. The upright, vigorous tree tends toward alternate bearing.

'PONKAN'

Also called Chinese honey mandarin and widely grown in other countries, 'Ponkan' is quite cold-hardy, with a tendency toward alternate bearing. Its somewhat seedy, very sweet fruit ripens in early winter.

SATSUMA

The earliest to ripen of mandarins (the fruit begins maturing in fall), satsumas are also the most cold-tolerant of all varieties listed here: mature plants have survived to 15°F/ −9°C without serious injury. The small trees are a fixture along the upper Gulf Coast and in other areas too cold for most mandarins; they produce poorly in the desert and in warm-winter parts of Florida.

The fruit has an orange, very loose rind and juicy, virtually seedless flesh with a mild, sweet flavor. It deteriorates quickly on the tree after ripening but keeps well in cool storage.

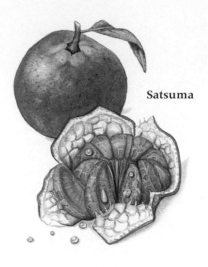

Satsuma

Several satsuma varieties are available, though 'Owari' is the main type offered in nurseries. 'Silverhill', a selection of 'Owari' sold in Florida, is thought to be identical to the 'Frost' satsuma sold in California. 'Dobashi Beni' and 'Okitsu Wase' ripen 2 to 3 weeks earlier than 'Owari'. 'Kimbrough' is a satsuma developed in Louisiana.

'WILKING'

Like other crosses between 'Mediterranean' and 'King', this rounded tree with willowlike leaves has a strong tendency toward alternate bearing. From winter into spring, it produces small to mediumsize fruit with a relatively thin rind. The very juicy flesh has a rich, distinctive flavor. The fruit stores fairly well on the tree, though it does get a little puffy once it's ripe.

Mandarin Hybrids

These citrus oddities—crosses involving mandarins and sweet oranges or grapefruit—date back to a rash of breeding conducted in Florida in the early 1900s. Some of the resulting varieties became classics; others fell by the wayside. Hybrids based on the previous generation are occasionally released even today. Time is usually the arbiter of success.

Like true mandarins, these hybrids peel fairly easily and are so delectable they should be enjoyed fresh.

Tangelo

A tangelo is a cross between a mandarin and a grapefruit.

The "tang" is short for "tangerine," a popular name for mandarins. The "elo" comes from "pummelo," a term the citrus industry of the time was encouraging consumers to use instead of "grapefruit."

Smaller and less dense in structure than grapefruit trees, tangelos are best suited to hot climates. They bear more plentiful—but seedier—fruit if a mandarin or tangor (see at right) is planted nearby for cross-pollination.

'Minneola'

This winter-bearing cross between 'Dancy' mandarin and 'Duncan' grapefruit bears large, bright orange-red, slightly seedy fruit, often with a prominent neck at the stem end. The flavor is rich and pleasingly tart.

'Orlando'

This variety has the same parents as 'Minneola'. The tree is

'Minneola' tangelo

similar in appearance except for its cupped leaves, but the fruit looks like a flattened orange and ripens about a month earlier than that of 'Minneola'. The mild, sweet flesh is very juicy, pale orange, and fairly seedy.

Tangor

The tangor is a hybrid between a mandarin and a sweet orange; it's often mislabeled as an orange when sold in grocery stores. The three tangors described here are thought to be naturally occurring hybrids rather than breeder-developed varieties. The plants are especially well adapted to areas of Florida favoring sweet oranges.

'Murcott'

This vigorous, upright tree produces medium-size, yellowish orange, thin-skinned, seedy fruit from late winter into spring. The flavor is so sweet that the fruit is marketed under the name Honey tangerine. Like many mandarins, 'Murcott' tends to bear heavily in alternate years.

'Ortanique'

A big, spreading tree, 'Ortanique' is a late ripener, maturing at about the same time as 'Valencia' orange. The fruit is medium-size, slightly flattened, and deep orange in color; it sometimes has a small navel. The sweet, juicy flesh may have few or many seeds.

'Temple'

This spreading, thorny, fairly cold-sensitive plant bears its crop in winter to spring. The large, flattened fruit, excellent for eating fresh or juicing, has a deep orange rind and seedy, sweet to tart flesh.

'Temple' is a superb performer in Florida but can also be grown in the desert. In the more moderate climates of the West, the flavor is too acidic.

OTHER HYBRIDS

Most of the hybrids included here resulted from crosses between mandarins and tangelos. The majority of these are commonly thought of as mandarins. Some varieties produce bigger or better (albeit seedier) crops when another variety with concurrent bloom is planted nearby for cross-pollination. 'Dancy' mandarin, 'Orlando' tangelo, and 'Temple' tangor are often used as pollinators.

'Murcott' tangor

'Ambersweet'

Classified as an orange for marketing purposes, this recently released variety is the result of crossing a hybrid of 'Clementine' mandarin and 'Orlando' tangelo with a mid-season orange.

From fall into winter, the dense, upright tree bears fruit that looks like a medium-size orange and is excellent for juicing. 'Ambersweet' doesn't need cross-pollination and becomes very seedy when grown near another variety.

'Fairchild'

This small, compact, winter-bearing hybrid between 'Clementine' mandarin and 'Orlando' tangelo is best suited to the desert, though it also produces good crops in South Texas and moderate climates of California. The fruit has a deep orange rind and juicy, richly sweet flesh. A pollinator improves yields.

'Fallglo'

Among the most recently released varieties, 'Fallglo' is the offspring of 'Temple' tangor and another citrus hybrid called 'Bower'. It bears its crop in mid to late fall, producing large, flattened fruit with a dark orange rind and tart, juicy, very seedy flesh. Yields are higher if a pollinator is grown nearby.

'Lee'

Developed at the same time as 'Osceola' and 'Robinson', this hybrid was thought to have the same parents as well: 'Clementine' mandarin and 'Orlando' tangelo. It was later discovered that the pollen had come not from 'Orlando' but from some other, unknown source.

'Lee' produces good-size, fairly seedy, low-acid fruit that ripens in late fall or early winter. The fruit attains the best flavor in Florida, though the variety isn't widely grown there.

'Nova'

Another cross between 'Clementine' mandarin and 'Orlando' tangelo, 'Nova' was released several years after 'Osceola' and 'Robinson'. It's a vigorous, thorny tree with big, flattened fruit that is marketed as a tangelo.

At one time, growers hoped that 'Nova' would rival 'Minneola' and 'Orlando'. That promise has not been fulfilled, but the juicy, richly sweet fruit, which ripens in late fall to early winter, is nonetheless well worth growing. The plant requires a pollinator.

'Osceola'

This plant was developed at the same time and from the same parents as 'Robinson'—and like 'Robinson', it's a fall-bearing tree that needs a pollinator. However, the small, bright orange fruit isn't as tasty as that of 'Robinson' and has never achieved popularity, not even in its home state of Florida.

'Page'

This cross between 'Clementine' mandarin and 'Minneola' tangelo is a vigorous plant that bears profusely from mid to late fall into winter. Though considered too small for the commercial market, the thin-skinned, juicy, richly sweet, nearly seedless fruit is still an excellent choice for the home garden. A pollinator only partly resolves the problem of undersized fruit.

'Robinson'

This fall-bearing offspring of 'Clementine' mandarin and 'Orlando' tangelo produces thin-skinned, deep orange, very sweet fruit that is susceptible to splitting. With a pollinator, the fruit can be quite seedy.

This variety grows best in Florida. It will also succeed in California, though not in the desert.

'Sunburst'

A relatively recent cross between 'Robinson' and 'Osceola', this variety bears big, red-orange, thin-skinned, sweet fruit in late fall. Florida-grown fruit has the richest flavor. 'Sunburst' is nearly seedless; yields are low

without cross-pollination from another variety.

'Wekiwa'

Not a widely available plant, 'Wekiwa' is a tangelolo—a cross between a tangelo (mandarin × grapefruit) and a grapefruit. Though it looks like a yellow-skinned, undersized grapefruit, it's peeled and eaten like a mandarin.

In high heat, the juicy, mildly sweet flesh is a light purplish rose color—hence the plant's other names, pink tangelo and 'Lavender Gem'. When grown in moderate to cool climates, however, it looks like a white-fleshed grapefruit. The fruit ripens from late fall into winter.

CITRUS WINE SPLASHES

About 2 cups chilled Asti Spumante; or use 2 cups brut or extra-dry champagne

About 2 cups fresh tangelo juice, juice of another mandarin hybrid, blood orange juice, or grapefruit juice

For each serving, pour about ⅓ cup wine into a wineglass; add about ⅓ cup citrus juice and stir gently. Makes 6 servings.

Sour-acid Mandarin

Most mandarins are deliciously sweet and meant to be eaten fresh—but these types are distinctly acidic. The two plants described here do produce useful fruit, but their main contribution is good looks. Attractive and fairly compact, they thrive outdoors in the ground or in pots; they'll even tolerate clipping into hedges, though at the expense of colorful fruit. As indoor plants, they're both decorative and reliably fruit-bearing.

Calamondin

This very cold-tolerant mandarin-kumquat hybrid is widely grown in Asia. It's especially popular in the Philippines, where it's called calamonding or kalamansi and raised for the tangy fruit that resembles a very small, slightly flattened orange. The easy-to-peel rind is sweet and edible, thanks to the plant's kumquat heritage; the juicy, slightly seedy flesh makes a tart flavoring. In the United States, calamondin is primarily used as an ornamental. The bright orange fruit, delicious in marmalades and ades, is a dividend.

Dense, upright, and nearly thornless, calamondin can reach over 25 feet tall, but as a standard tree it seldom exceeds 15 feet. A variegated form with green-and-white foliage is available; its fruit is green-striped when immature, ripening to an overall yellow-orange.

Calamondin is very showy when laden with fruit—and it's nearly everbearing in mild regions. The fruit stores on the tree for many months.

Because it's the citrus that fruits the best indoors, calamondin is a valued houseplant in cold-winter climates. Often sold as a rooted cutting, it can prosper in an 8- to 10-inch container for years.

'Rangpur'

Though commonly called 'Rangpur' lime, this native of India—often used as a rootstock for other citrus—is not a true lime, nor does it taste like one. The acidic juice can, however, be substituted for lime juice. Its complex flavor also makes it a rich, interesting base for punches and mixed drinks.

Everbearing in mild climates, 'Rangpur' produces a profusion of reddish orange fruit that hangs on all year. The small to medium-size, rounded fruit looks and peels like a mandarin. The deep orange, seedy flesh is very juicy.

A fairly hardy plant with a bushy, spreading, drooping habit and few thorns, 'Rangpur' grows quickly to about 15 feet high and wide. It may be budded onto another rootstock or offered as a rooted cutting.

'Otaheite', also called Tahiti orange, is an acidless form sold as a houseplant by mail-order nurseries. It is less vigorous than 'Rangpur' and thus dwarfed. Though the fruit has a limelike scent, the flavor is usually described as insipid.

Variegated calamondin

PUMMELO

Another name for this big-fruited forerunner of the grapefruit is "shaddock," after a Captain Shaddock, an English seaman who brought the plant to Barbados in the late 17th century. The pummelo originated in Asia, though, and that's where it is still most widely grown and appreciated.

Pummelos are large-leafed, big-flowered plants that vary in size. Most of the varieties grown in the United States are smaller than grapefruit trees, though those cultivated in Florida are as large or larger. All types bear clusters of enormous round to pear-shaped fruit with very thick rind and pith—once peeled, the fruit is just slightly bigger than a grapefruit.

Like grapefruit, pummelos come in white- and rosy-fleshed varieties, though there isn't a typical flavor as there is for grapefruit. To get an idea of the range, visit a market in any American city with a sizable Asian population: you'll find different types of pummelos with flavors from sweet to fairly acidic.

The firm flesh isn't as juicy as that of a grapefruit,

'Chandler'

and each segment is encased in a tough membrane. To eat a pummelo, peel the fruit, pull the segments apart, and remove the pulp from its casing. Pummelos tend to be seedy if raised near other citrus; when grown in isolation, most types contain few or no seeds.

Pummelos are about as hardy as grapefruit but need a little less heat to ripen. Like rosy-fleshed grapefruit, the pigmented kinds color up best in high heat. The fruit ripens in early winter in the warmest-summer areas, but it doesn't mature until early spring in cooler climates. It holds on the tree for several months without appreciable loss of quality.

Pummelo trees are being offered by an increasing number of nurseries on the West Coast and in other areas where Asian immigrants have settled. The plants haven't yet attracted much notice in Texas and Florida, where grapefruit is king.

'CHANDLER'

The most widely available variety, this round-fruited pummelo has sweet pink flesh. A hybrid developed in California, it's a vigorous plant with an open growth habit that allows easy espaliering.

'HIRADO BUNTAN'

The sweetest and best-tasting of the pink-fleshed varieties tested in Florida, this large plant originated as a seedling of a Japanese white-fleshed pummelo. The fruit is round to slightly flattened.

'REINKING'

Another hybrid from California, 'Reinking' produces bigger fruit than 'Chandler', on a slightly larger, denser tree. The pear-shaped, white-fleshed fruit isn't as sweet as that of 'Chandler', though.

'TAHITIAN'

This variety is also known as 'Sarawak', for the region of Borneo where it is thought to have originated. The trees are small; the large, pear-shaped, white-fleshed fruit is moderately acidic, with a lime undertone.

GRAPEFRUIT

'Flame'

Among the largest citrus trees (standards grow to about 30 feet tall), the grapefruit is so named because it bears its crop in grapelike clusters among the large, dark green leaves.

Grapefruit trees are fairly cold-sensitive, and the fruit needs heat to develop its luscious sweet-tart flavor. Though good crops can be grown in the desert, the best grapefruit comes from Florida and Texas, where the plant enjoys ideal conditions: summers with hot days, warm nights, and humidity above 60 percent, and winters with sunny days and coolish nights. Commercially, two favored locales are Florida's Indian River region and Texas's Lower Rio Grande Valley.

The fruit can ripen in as little as 6 months for fall and winter harvest, but ripening can also take a year or longer, in which case the tree will bear overlapping crops. As long as the fruit gets the total required heat, it doesn't matter whether the warmth comes quickly or slowly. However, the longer the ripening process, the greater the chance of cold damage in freeze-prone areas.

In cool-summer regions, where true grapefruit tends to be thick-skinned and bitter, the grapefruit-pummelo hybrids 'Melogold' and 'Oroblanco' are a breakthrough. They look and taste much like grapefruit, yet require less heat.

First described in the mid-18th century, the grapefruit is believed to be a mutation from the pummelos (see page 77) grown in the West Indies; at first, it was known as the "forbidden fruit." It arrived on American shores in the 1820s, when a French settler from the Bahamas planted it on Tampa Bay. All modern grapefruit raised in the U. S. today are descended from this planting.

Depending on the variety, grapefruit may have so-called white (actually pale yellow) or rosy flesh. Though red pigmentation doesn't indicate a different flavor (as it does in blood oranges versus other sweet oranges, for example), breeders—especially those in Texas—have labored long and hard to produce fruit with rich, long-lasting color. The pigment develops only in prolonged high heat; where summers are cool, however, the flesh of a red grapefruit may appear white.

Grapefruit has multiple uses. Eat it fresh as an appetizer or dessert, slice it into salads, juice it, or turn it into marmalade or candied peel. Though most varieties are called "seedless," you can expect at least a few seeds.

'DUNCAN'

This granddaddy of grapefruit varieties was among the first cultivated in Florida. It's still grown primarily in that state

BROILED GRAPEFRUIT

- 1 grapefruit, cut into halves
- 2 to 3 tablespoons firmly packed brown sugar
- 1 to 2 teaspoons orange-flavored liqueur (optional)

Remove and discard seeds from grapefruit. Place grapefruit halves, cut side up, in a small, shallow baking pan. Press brown sugar through a wire strainer to cover tops of grapefruit evenly. Then broil grapefruit about 4 inches below heat just until sugar is bubbly (about 2 minutes). Drizzle with liqueur, if desired; serve hot for brunch or a light dessert. Makes 2 servings.

and bears slightly larger fruit than modern varieties. Even though its flavor is considered superior to that of the newer, seedless types, seediness (30 to 50 seeds per fruit!) keeps 'Duncan' out of produce bins. Instead, it's processed for juice and sections.

'FLAME'

A seedling selection of 'Henderson', this is the variety now being most widely planted in Florida. It has red flesh comparable to that of 'Rio Red', a slight rind blush, and few to no seeds.

'MARSH'

Sometimes called 'Marsh Seedless', this seedling of 'Duncan' is the main white-fleshed commercial variety. It gave rise to a pigmented version called 'Pink Marsh' ('Thompson')—not as popular as some of the newer, more highly colored varieties, since the slightly pink flesh fades as the season progresses.

'MELOGOLD'

This white-fleshed hybrid is the result of a cross between a grapefruit and an acidless pummelo. The fruit drops much sooner than true grapefruit, which will hang on the tree for a year or more.

'Melogold' bears typically completely seedless fruit which is bigger, thinner-skinned, and sweeter than that of 'Oroblanco', another hybrid. The plant is a little more cold-sensitive than 'Oroblanco'.

'OROBLANCO'

This almost to entirely seedless grapefruit-pummelo hybrid has the same parents as 'Melogold', but its rind is thicker and its white flesh is more sweet-tart in flavor. The fruit matures a month or so before that of 'Melogold'. Like 'Melogold', 'Oroblanco' drops its fruit sooner than a true grapefruit.

'RAY RUBY' AND 'HENDERSON'

These virtually indistinguishable seedless varieties have nearly the rind blush but not quite the flesh pigmentation of 'Rio Red'. The flesh color holds, even late in the season.

'REDBLUSH'

Also known as 'Ruby' and 'Ruby Red', this seedless variety is a sport of 'Pink Marsh'. The rind is red-tinted. The flesh is red but doesn't hold its color, fading to pink by midseason, to buff later on.

'RIO RED'

Developed from 'Redblush' and released in the 1980s, this seedless variety has a deeper rind color than 'Ray Ruby' and 'Henderson'. It isn't quite as red-fleshed as 'Star Ruby', but it's a more reliable fruit producer.

'STAR RUBY'

On the plus side, this seedless variety is the reddest of all those listed here—and the intense color holds even late in the season. There are some minuses, too, however; growers have reported problems such as erratic bearing and greater propensity to cold damage. 'Star Ruby' doesn't hold up well to desert heat.

'Melogold'

LEMON

Indispensable in kitchens the world over, this sour-fruited citrus is thought to have originated in India. It was introduced to Europe in the 12th century by Arab traders, then brought to the New World by Columbus.

A low heat requirement makes lemons a wonderful choice for regions where sweet oranges and grapefruit won't ripen. The trees thrive in cool-summer areas of the citrus belt and will even produce fruit indoors in northern climes. Yet they withstand high temperatures too, bearing successfully in desert heat.

Lemon trees are especially suited to dry-summer regions of the West—in fact, most of

'Eureka'

the commercial crop is produced in California. You can expect lemons from the humid subtropics to be much bigger than those sold in grocery stores.

True lemons (some varieties are hybrids) are quite susceptible to cold, though they aren't as sensitive as limes. They're vigorous plants that don't dwarf well, so figure on a mature height of 20 to 25 feet. Also keep in mind that they'll need pruning every now and then.

In mild climates, lemons produce their purple-tinted white blossoms all year, and it's not unusual to see fruit at different stages of ripeness on the tree at the same time. In intense heat, plants tend to produce a single crop late in the year.

Lemons can be harvested as soon as they're juicy, even if the rind is still green. Don't leave fruit on the tree too long after it turns yellow; if you do, it will lose flavor and get pithy.

Lemon juice and peel are used as flavorings and in cooking and baking. The tangy juice is also a favorite for ades and other beverages.

'BEARSS'

Grown in Florida, this thorny, vigorous true lemon is a selec-

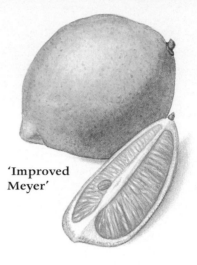

'Improved Meyer'

tion of a Sicilian variety—and quite different from 'Bearss' lime. Its fruit is similar to that of 'Eureka'.

'EUREKA'

You don't have to be a gardener to know this lemon—it's the most common market variety. The somewhat thick-skinned fruit is oblong in shape, with a nipple at one end; the flesh is highly acidic, with few seeds.

'Eureka' has long, nearly thornless shoots that make it a good candidate for espalier. It isn't quite as vigorous or cold-resistant as 'Lisbon', the other true lemon widely grown in the West.

'IMPROVED MEYER'

This hybrid between a lemon and a sweet orange or mandarin is a favorite among home gardeners. Not only does the plant withstand more cold than a true lemon, but it's much smaller (it can reach 15 feet but generally stays lower) and needs no pruning to keep it in bounds. It has few thorns.

The fruit of 'Improved Meyer' is quite different from that of a true lemon: it's nearly round, fairly thin-skinned, and orange-tinged throughout. The very juicy, mild flesh contains few seeds. Though the flavor is less acidic than that of a true lemon, the juice is still delicious in pies and ades.

'Improved Meyer' replaced 'Meyer', which carried tristeza virus, a serious disease affecting citrus. Neither variety is legal in Arizona, though. The plants may be budded onto another root-stock or sold as rooted cuttings; they take well to hedging and thrive in pots.

'LISBON'

The fruit of this true lemon is very similar to that of 'Eureka' and is also sold in markets, but the trees differ. 'Lisbon' is more vigorous and a little larger, with denser, thornier growth; it's also a bit more frost-tolerant.

Along with its selection 'Seedless Lisbon'—identical aside from its lack of seeds—this is the preferred lemon for desert gardens, since its fruit is borne inside the canopy, where it is shielded from the elements.

'PONDEROSA'

Catalog companies tout this lemon-citron hybrid as the American Wonder: it bears grapefruit-size fruit weighing up to 2 pounds apiece! The acidic pulp beneath the thick, bumpy rind is seedy and only moderately juicy, but it's perfectly acceptable for cooking and baking.

'Ponderosa' is even more cold-sensitive than a true lemon and is generally grown indoors as a novelty. A natural dwarf often sold as a rooted cutting, it flourishes in containers. Though thorny, it's also easy to espalier.

'VARIEGATED PINK'

Also called 'Pink Lemonade', this is a sport of 'Eureka' and is similarly frost-tender. Both leaves and fruit are variegated. The green-and-white foliage, which emerges purple-tinged, is handsome all year. The lemons are green-striped when immature; the stripes fade as the fruit ripens to yellow. The very tart, nearly seedless, light pink flesh does not need intense heat or cool nighttime temperatures to develop color. The pinker the pulp, the less acidic the flavor—so harvest the fruit when it has the flavor you want, regardless of how deep the flesh color is.

'Variegated Pink' tends to be much smaller than 'Eureka', generally growing to about 8 feet tall. It's a handsome container plant.

'Variegated Pink'

FROSTY LEMONADE OR LIMEADE

1 cup fresh lemon or lime juice
¾ cup sugar
4 cups cold water
   Crushed ice or ice cubes
   Lemon or lime slices (optional)

In a pitcher, combine lemon juice and sugar; stir until sugar is dissolved. Add water and mix well. To serve, pour into ice-filled glasses; garnish with lemon slices, if desired. Makes about 1½ quarts.

LIME

The common sour-fruited limes look enough like lemons that they're marketed green to avoid confusing consumers—but if you sample both fruits, there's no mistaking the lime's distinctive tang. Though limes left on the tree turn yellow, ripeness is determined not by rind color but by the juiciness of the fruit.

There's a lime for just about every area of the citrus belt warm enough for sweet oranges. These plants thrive in hot, humid regions like Florida, where they outperform lemons; they can also be grown in the desert and in more moderate regions of California. Available varieties range from moderately to extremely cold-sensitive, with fruit varying from intensely sour to nearly devoid of acid.

Historical references to limes appear later than do those to lemons. A 13th-century Arab writer described a fruit something like a lime, but it wasn't until four centuries later that an English author mentioned the fruit by name.

Some former uses for limes might strike us as a bit unusual today. In 18th-century France, for example, court ladies used the fruit as a sort of cosmetic, carrying it with them and biting into it to redden their lips. On British ships, lime juice was served as a scurvy-preventative on long ocean voyages—hence the nickname "limey" for British sailors (and, by extension, for Britons in general).

Today, we tend to rely on lipstick and vitamin C pills for rosy lips and good health—but the various limes are still splendid as a seasoning, in cooking and baking, and in ades and mixed drinks.

'BEARSS' OR 'PERSIAN'

This large-fruited lime, the main variety sold in grocery stores, may actually be a hybrid between a lime and a lemon or citron. It's known as 'Bearss' in the West, as 'Persian' (or sometimes 'Tahiti') in Florida and Texas.

Most Western gardeners will have better success with this variety than with 'Mexican' lime, since the former needs less heat for fruiting and is several degrees hardier. The small-thorned plant is rather open in structure when young, but becomes dense and rounded at maturity. It eventually reaches about 15 to 20 feet tall. The fruit is nearly the size of a true lemon. The thin, medium green rind turns pale yellow when the fruit is allowed to ripen on the tree; the greenish yellow, acidic flesh is seedless.

In the hottest areas, this variety tends to produce primarily in summer. In milder climates, fruiting occurs during much of the year.

'KIEFFER'

Popular in Thai and Cambodian cooking, 'Kieffer' lime has become available in California due to the demand from Asian immigrants. You may see the names 'Kaffir' and 'Kuffre'; other appellations include Indonesian lime and Makrut lime. The plant is often sold under its botanical name, *Citrus hystrix*.

'Kieffer'

"Bearss' and 'Mexican'

In spring, the frost-tender, thorny shrub produces small, rounded fruit with seedy, sour, light green flesh and a bumpy, dark green rind that looks like alligator hide. The elongated, notched leaves are used as a flavoring, as are the rind and scant juice.

'MEXICAN'

High heat demand and near-zero tolerance for frost make this small-fruited, acid lime best suited to the warmest regions. In more moderate climates, find a hot planting spot or grow the tree in a container and shelter it during cold spells.

'Mexican' lime is also known as bartender's lime and West Indian lime; another name is 'Key' lime, a reference to the fact that the trees were once grown commercially in the Florida Keys. The basic variety is a twiggy, very thorny plant to about 15 feet high; 'Mexican Thornless', a spine-free selection with fruit identical to that of 'Mexican', is also available. The trees are everbearing, and limes at various stages of ripeness are often seen on the same plant. About an inch in diameter at maturity, the rounded fruit has a thin, medium green rind; once the rind turns yellow, the fruit tends to drop. The highly acidic, somewhat seedy flesh is yellowish green.

Connoisseurs consider this lime superior to 'Bearss' or 'Persian'. Its complex, sour flavor is preferred for Key lime pie and mixed drinks.

'PALESTINE SWEET'

Also called Indian lime, this variety produces an acidless fruit, often described as insipid by those accustomed to sour limes. It's popular in Middle Eastern, Indian, and Latin American cooking, and requests from immigrants have made it available in many parts of California.

Quite cold-sensitive, the thorny, shrubby plant bears a single crop in fall or winter. About the same size and shape as 'Bearss' or 'Persian' lime, the thin-skinned fruit turns from greenish to orange-yellow with ripening. The flesh is yellow and very juicy.

'RANGPUR'

Though commonly labeled 'Rangpur' lime, this is actually a sour-acid mandarin. See page 76.

· ·
QUICK LIME CURD

2 teaspoons grated lime peel
⅓ cup fresh lime juice
2 large eggs
1 large egg yolk
½ cup sugar
¼ cup butter or margarine, melted

In a blender or food processor, combine lime peel, lime juice, eggs, egg yolk, and sugar. Whirl until well blended. With motor running, add butter in a thin stream. Transfer mixture to a 1- to 2-quart non-aluminum pan.

Cook over low heat, stirring constantly, until mixture is thick enough to mound slightly when dropped from a spoon (6 to 8 minutes). Refrigerate until cold (or for up to 2 weeks) before serving. Serve as you would jam, as a spread for biscuits, toast, or scones. Makes about 1 cup.

KUMQUAT

'Meiwa'

Long grown in Asia, the kumquat is now enjoying increased popularity in the United States—not only in home gardens, where it's favored for its hardiness and showy, palatable fruit, but also in grocery stores, where Asian immigrants have created a demand for it.

The Chinese have appreciated kumquats for centuries, enjoying the fruit at banquets and displaying it in centerpieces and bouquets. A 12th-century writer described the fruit as glistening like golden bullets. Today, the kumquat is known as a good-luck plant, and dwarf trees or fruiting branches are popular gifts during the Chinese New Year. The Japanese also use kumquats for holiday decorations.

The kumquat was introduced to Europe in 1846 by the English plant hunter Robert Fortune. In his honor, it was given a separate classification, *Fortunella,* rather than being grouped scientifically with other citrus fruits.

Attractive, densely branched, and shrubby, the kumquat typically has few or no thorns. It's lovely as a specimen, foundation, or container plant; it also tolerates clipping into a fairly low hedge. When grown on their own roots, plants vary in size from about 6 to over 15 feet tall; grown on a dwarfing rootstock, they rarely exceed 4 feet.

Kumquats bear richly perfumed white blossoms that develop into a wealth of yellow to bright reddish orange fruit. The fruits resemble tiny oranges, but they're eaten whole and unpeeled; the

spongy rind is the sweet part, while the pulp is tangy and not very juicy.

Plants grow actively only when temperatures are relatively high, so the best fruiting occurs in areas with warm to hot summers. Yet heat is only half the story: nighttime chill (temperatures below 50°F/10°C) is essential during the ripening process for good color and flavor.

The fruit starts to ripen in mid-fall in the warmest climates, but it doesn't mature until late winter in cooler regions. It can hang on the plant for up to a year without any decrease in quality.

Since kumquats start blooming later in the year than most citrus and stop growing earlier in fall, they're ideal for the northernmost limits of the citrus belt. Mature plants are said to be hardy to 18°F/−8°C, but thanks to their extended dormant period, they can actual-

'Nagami'

ly endure lower temperatures—perhaps to 10°F/−12°C. The fruit, however, is just as vulnerable to cold as that of other citrus.

Because the kumquat is so hardy, scientists have used it to breed what they hoped would be other types of cold-tolerant citrus with tasty fruit; see the discussion of limequats and orangequats on page 86.

Kumquats are extremely versatile. Eat them whole or sliced into salads; candy them, bake them into breads, or turn them into jams, pie fillings, or chutney. Or use them in sauces for duck, lamb, and other poultry and meats.

'HONG KONG'

Also called golden bean, this very thorny plant grows wild on hillsides in Hong Kong. It's strictly ornamental; the pea-size, big-seeded fruit is sour and virtually inedible.

'MARUMI'

Grown mainly in Florida, this slightly thorny kumquat bears round fruit that is smaller than that of 'Meiwa' and typically contains a few seeds. The peel is sweeter than that of 'Nagami', though the pulp is more acidic.

'MEIWA'

The round fruit of this nearly thornless kumquat is considered the best for eating fresh—it's bigger, sweeter, juicier, and less seedy than fruit borne by either 'Nagami' or 'Marumi'. This variety is also better able to produce sweet fruit in cool, coastal climates.

'NAGAMI'

First brought to this country from China in the mid-1800s, the oval-fruited, slightly seedy 'Nagami' is the main commercial kumquat variety. It produces more abundant and sweeter fruit in hot-summer climates than it does in cooler areas. The thornless plant is easy to espalier.

KUMQUAT MERINGUE PIE

1 to 1¼ pounds (3 to 4 cups) kumquats
6 tablespoons cornstarch
1½ cups sugar
1½ cups water
4 large eggs, separated
3 tablespoons butter or margarine
Baked pastry shell for a single-crust 9-inch pie
½ teaspoon vanilla

Thinly slice 6 kumquats; discard seeds from slices, then set slices aside.

Cut remaining kumquats in half and pinch between your fingers to squeeze out juice and pulp. Press juice-pulp mixture through a fine strainer into a bowl, then measure; you need ½ cup. Discard residue in strainer.

In a 3-quart non-aluminum pan, stir together cornstarch and 1¼ cups of the sugar. Gradually add water and the ½ cup kumquat juice, whisking until smooth. Then whisk over medium-high heat until mixture thickens and comes to a full boil. Remove from heat.

In a small bowl, beat egg yolks to blend. Whisk about ½ cup of the hot kumquat mixture into egg yolks; then whisk egg yolk mixture back into pan. Return to very low heat and cook, stirring, for 2 minutes. Remove from heat. Add butter and stir until melted; stir in sliced kumquats. Let cool slightly, then pour into pastry shell.

In a large bowl, beat egg whites with an electric mixer on high speed until frothy. Gradually add remaining ¼ cup sugar, 1 tablespoon at a time, beating until whites hold stiff, glossy peaks. Beat in vanilla. With a spatula, spread meringue over filling and up against edge of pastry; make decorative swirls in meringue, if desired. Bake pie in a 350° oven until peaks of meringue are lightly browned (12 to 15 minutes). Let cool for at least 3 hours (or up to 12 hours) before serving. Makes 8 servings.

KUMQUAT HYBRIDS

Since kumquats are so hardy, why not hybridize them to produce other types of cold-tolerant citrus? That was the idea behind a series of USDA experiments undertaken in Florida during the early 1900s. The most successful results of that work are the limequat and orangequat. Though neither fruit has become a commercial success, both are worthy of consideration by home gardeners.

These hybrids tend to be fairly small even as standards, and on a dwarfing rootstock they reach only 3 to 6 feet. Highly ornamental as foundation plants or in pots, they also bear an abundance of useful fruit.

LIMEQUAT

The result of crossing a kumquat with the extremely cold-susceptible 'Mexican' lime, the limequat bears fruit with the approximate flavor and aroma of lime. It's a little more frost-tolerant and requires less heat than its lime parent, though.

The fruit, which turns yellow when ripe, matures mainly from fall to spring, though some is produced all year.

You can use limequats in place of limes as a fresh flavoring and in cooking. One noteworthy difference: while limes have a bitter rind, limequats have inherited a sweet, edible skin from their kumquat parent.

'Eustis'

This limequat is the offspring of the round 'Marumi' kumquat; its fruit, which contains some small seeds, is about the shape and size of a jumbo olive. Shrubby and twiggy, the plant is a good choice for espalier, since it has pendulous branches.

'Tavares'

Nearly or entirely seedless, this newer variety has the largest fruit of any limequat variety. Its attractive, elongated oval shape recalls the fruit of its kumquat parent, 'Nagami'.

'Tavares' is a more compact, fuller, and shapelier plant than 'Eustis'.

ORANGEQUAT

A compact, handsome plant, the orangequat produces deep orange fruit a little larger than a kumquat that can be eaten skin and all. The rind is sweet, the pulp juicy and slightly acidic; the overall flavor is sweeter than that of a kumquat.

The most widely available orangequat variety is 'Nippon', a cross between the large round 'Meiwa' kumquat and a satsuma mandarin. Both of its parents are quite cold-tolerant; the orangequat's hardiness range falls somewhere between the two.

Orangequats have a fairly low heat requirement for ripening fruit. They produce in two main cycles—the first in winter, the second in spring—but the fruit stores on the tree for months.

Use orangequats fresh or make them into marmalade, chutney, or candied fruit.

'Tavares' limequat

'Nippon' orangequat

CITRON

'Buddha's Hand'

The first type of citrus to be cultivated, the citron originated in the Himalayan region and was brought to the Middle East by the Medes around the 7th century B.C. It was probably the only citrus known in ancient Greece and Rome, where the fragrant fruit was used as a room perfumant and moth repellent. Today, we're most familiar with citron as a candied fruit—but this use arose only after sugar had become widely available.

It is thought that the words "citron" and "citrus" are related to the Greek *kedros,* meaning "cedar"; the citron fruit supposedly resembled a cedar cone.

The plant itself isn't very ornamental: it's small, thorny, irregular in shape, and rather straggly. Its claim to fame is the big, thick-skinned yellow fruit it bears throughout the year, with the main harvest in fall. Only the rind is used—candied, made into marmalade, blended into teas, or eaten fresh in salads.

Citron is relatively short-lived and extremely sensitive to cold. The foliage is usually damaged at the freezing point; the fruit is a few degrees hardier. If grown in the ground, the plants are best restricted to normally frost-free areas, though they can freeze to the ground and come back (as has been the case in South Texas). To be on the safe side, grow citron in containers and move it to a protected site in cold weather.

The plants are often sold as cuttings, since they grow well on their own roots.

'BUDDHA'S HAND'

The unusual fruit is sometimes referred to as a fingered citron, since it's divided into fingerlike sections at one end. It has also been likened to an octopus or a bunch of gnarled bananas. The fruit contains no pulp, just rind.

'Buddha's Hand' is a symbol of supreme happiness in Buddhism and other Asian religions, and its image is often found in jade carvings of all sorts. Extremely fragrant, the fruit is still used as a perfumant in Asia. In the United States, the plant is usually grown as a novelty.

'ETROG'

The fruit of 'Etrog' is shaped like an oversized lemon, with ridges along the length of its rough, warty rind. The acidic pulp is so dry that it has no practical use.

This citron is thought to be the "hadar" fruit mentioned in the Bible. It has been used since early times in the Jewish Feast of the Tabernacles (Succoth).

'Etrog'

Hardy Citrus

'Flying Dragon' trifoliate orange

Home gardeners living just beyond the citrus belt have long searched for exceptionally cold-tolerant citrus with palatable fruit. Although flavor matches for sweet oranges and grapefruit have yet to be found, the hardy varieties cited here are well worth trying. These types as well as other good selections are available through the sources listed on the facing page.

The plants we describe are good choices for USDA zone 8 and warm areas of zone 7; some can be grown in even chillier regions. The hardiness figures apply to established, fully dormant plants that have been conditioned to cold by the time freezes arrive.

Australian Razzelquat

A shrubby, tiny-leafed plant that grows well in very dry climates and humid conditions alike, the razzelquat bears small, round, yellow-skinned fruit about 3 months after spring flowering. The pulpy, sweet-tart fruit, which is eaten skin and all, tastes like lemon or lime candy. It also makes good jam.

Though not as hardy as some other varieties listed here, the razzelquat survives easily to 14°F/–10°C—and will take even more cold if given some protection.

'Changsha' Mandarin

From fall into winter, this old Chinese variety produces orange-skinned fruit resembling a satsuma. The juicy, seedy flesh is fairly tasty, but the fruit doesn't hold well on the tree, drying out quickly when fully ripe.

Hardy to about 5°F/–15°C, the small trees are often grown in those parts of Texas, the Gulf Coast, and the Southwest where conditions are too cold for conventional mandarin varieties.

Citrange

Hybrids between a sweet orange and trifoliate orange, citranges are small trees commonly used as rootstocks in citrus country. In colder climates, some types are grown for their fruit, tasty enough to be eaten fresh or used for juice or marmalade.

For nearly a century, 'Morton' came closest to a sweet orange, though its flavor is somewhat tart. A recently released variety, 'US-119', is sweeter. Both kinds form large, juicy fruit with few to no seeds and ripen in late fall, with 'US-119' maturing a few weeks later than 'Morton'. The plants are hardy to between 10°F/–12°C and 5°F/–15°C.

Ichang Papeda

Also called Ichang lemon, this shrub or small tree from the highlands of China is reportedly hardy to subzero temperatures. Starting early in fall, it bears rounded, pale yellow, lemon-sized fruit with a bumpy rind, juicy flesh, and big seeds. Use it the same way you'd use lemons.

Khasi Papeda

A small tree from India, Khasi papeda bears its grapefruit-size fruit a couple of weeks later than Ichang papeda. The flesh, which has an unusual peppery tang, can be eaten fresh in segments or squeezed for juice. The plant easily survives to 15°F/–9°C and has been reported to withstand considerably more cold.

NANSHO DAIDAI

Hardy to about 0°F/–18°C, this tough, thorny tree bears big, bright orange fruit in fall. The very sour, seedy flesh is spooned from the rind like grapefruit, though most people would want to sprinkle it with sugar before eating. When sweetened, the juice is quite drinkable.

'THOMASVILLE' CITRANGEQUAT

The citrangequat was developed in an effort to combine the cold hardiness of a trifoliate orange and kumquat with the good eating quality of a sweet orange. The resulting plants are hardy to about 0°F/–18°C.

'Thomasville', an attractive variety from Georgia, develops small, nearly seedless, acidic "oranges" in fall. Harvested while sour, the fruit can be used as a lime substitute or made into marmalade; left on the tree for up to a year, it may become sweet enough to eat fresh.

TRIFOLIATE ORANGE

A common rootstock in the citrus belt, this spiny deciduous shrub or small tree is grown as an ornamental oddity or impenetrable hedge in regions with winter temperatures as low as –20°F/–29°C.

Big, fragrant blossoms appear in spring, followed by leaves consisting of three leaflets. Inedible, golf ball–size yellow fruit hangs on into winter, decorating the branches.

'Flying Dragon', a natural dwarf to about 6 feet tall, has contorted branches and long, curved thorns. It's hardy to about –15°F/–26°C.

'YUZU' ICHANDARIN

A natural mandarin hybrid grown commercially in Japan, 'Yuzu' ripens from fall into winter. Beneath the medium-size fruit's deep yellow, easy-to-peel rind is mildly sweet flesh with a lemon-lime flavor and big seeds. The fruit is eaten fresh and used as a seasoning and in baking.

The shrubby plant grows slowly to about 12 feet tall; it's hardy to about 0°F/–18°C.

SOURCES

The following mail-order sources sell the hardy citrus just described as well as more tender varieties for container growing. Keep in mind that citrus plants cannot be shipped to California, Arizona, Texas, Louisiana, or Florida.

Edible Landscaping
P.O. Box 77
Afton, VA 22920
(800) 524-4156

Northwoods Retail Nursery
27635 South Oglesby Road
Canby, OR 97013
(503) 266-5432

Oregon Exotics
Rare Fruit Nursery
1065 Messinger Road
Grants Pass, OR 97527
(503) 846-7578

Pacific Tree Farms
4301 Lynwood Drive
Chula Vista, CA 91910
(619) 422-2400

Raintree Nursery
391 Butts Road
Morton, WA 98356
(360) 496-6400

Woodlanders, Inc.
1128 Colleton Avenue
Aiken, SC 29801
(803) 648-7522

Citrus at a Glance

This chart briefly describes more than 80 citrus varieties and indicates the regions where they are best suited for year-round outdoor growing. You can, of course, try growing a variety out of its ideal range, but keep in mind that the plant may fruit poorly, fail to develop characteristic flavor or color, or need cold protection.

If you don't see a particular variety at local nurseries, ask whether it can be obtained. You may even want to take a stab at propagating it yourself; see pages 35 and 36.

For more information about the various types of citrus, refer to the entries in this chapter.

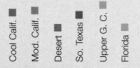

Calamondin

NAVEL ORANGE (SEE PAGES 65–66)

	Cool Calif.	Mod. Calif.	Desert	So. Texas	Upper G. C.	Florida	
'Cara Cara'		■	■	■		■	The first rosy-fleshed navel. Seedless flesh is red in Florida, pink in warm regions of California. An early navel, bearing from fall into winter, at about the same time as 'Washington'.
'Fukumoto'		■	■				Seedless fruit with excellent flavor and orange-red rind. Ripens about a week before 'Washington'.
'Lane Late'		■					Australian variety ripens 4 to 6 weeks after 'Washington'. Seedless.
'Robertson'		■					Clusters of seedless fruit mature 2 to 3 weeks earlier than 'Washington'. Dwarf versions are prolific bearers.
'Skaggs Bonanza'		■	■				Seedless fruit ripens about 2 weeks before 'Washington' but doesn't hold on the tree as long.
'Spring'		■					Newly introduced late navel from California ripens about the same time as 'Lane Late' but has bigger, more highly colored fruit. Seedless.
'Washington'		■	■	■		■	Main commercial navel and original variety from which other navels developed. High-quality, seedless eating orange ripens fall into winter and stores on the tree 3 to 4 months. In Texas and Florida, local selections sold simply as "navel" have better flavor than 'Washington'.

COMMON ORANGE (SEE PAGES 66–67)

	Cool Calif.	Mod. Calif.	Desert	So. Texas	Upper G. C.	Florida	
'Hamlin'			■	■		■	Early juice orange with low-acid, nearly seedless flesh ripens fall into winter. One of the "Arizona Sweets."
'Jaffa'		■	■	■			Midseason, nearly seedless eating orange from Israel ripens winter into spring. Excellent flavor.
'Marrs'			■	■			Early-ripening eating orange is a sport of 'Washington' but without a navel. Low-acid flesh has few seeds unless pollinated by nearby varieties. One of the "Arizona Sweets."
'Parson Brown'				■		■	Early-ripening small juice orange is flavorful but seedy. Best suited to Florida.
'Pineapple'			■	■		■	Leading midseason orange in Florida. Rich-flavored, fairly seedy fruit is excellent for juicing, tends to drop from the tree after ripening. Alternate bearer. One of the "Arizona Sweets."
'Trovita'	■	■	■				Midseason eating and juice orange with few seeds is a sport of 'Washington' without the navel. Develops good flavor not just in moderate climates but also in the desert and near the coast. One of the "Arizona Sweets."
'Valencia'	■	■	■	■		■	Late-season, nearly seedless juice orange ripens from midwinter in the hottest areas to summer in the coolest. 'Delta' and 'Midnight' are seedless selections maturing a little earlier. If grown in Florida, 'Rohde Red' has more highly colored flesh than the regular 'Valencia'. All types hold on the tree for months, improving in flavor.

■ Cool California = Coastal and other cool-summer areas of California   ■ Moderate California = Warm inland and coastal valleys of California
■ Desert = Low desert of California and low and intermediate deserts of Arizona   ■ South Texas = Lower Rio Grande Valley north to Corpus Christi

	Cool Calif.	Mod. Calif.	Desert	So. Texas	Upper G. C.	Florida	
BLOOD ORANGE (SEE PAGE 68)							
'Moro'	■	■	■				Red-blushed rind and deep burgundy, sweet-tart flesh with berry overtones. The only blood orange with good color and flavor in coastal Northern California. Also colors up well in the desert. Crop ripens winter to spring.
'Sanguinelli'		■	■				Rosy rind and sweet-tart orange flesh streaked with burgundy. Similar to 'Moro' in berry overtones and harvest time.
'Tarocco'		■	■				Red flesh but very little rind blush. Produces the most reliable color and sweetest, most berrylike flavor in warm inland valleys of California.
SOUR ORANGE (SEE PAGE 69)							
'Bouquet de Fleurs' ('Bouquet')	■	■	■	■	■	■	Beautiful spreading tree 8 to 10 feet high with fragrant blooms used by French perfume makers. Nearly seedless fruit ripens fall to winter and holds for a year.
'Chinotto' (Myrtle-leaf orange)	■	■	■	■	■	■	Attractive, compact tree to 7 feet or a little taller, with small, myrtlelike leaves and seedy fruit. Harvest time is the same as for 'Bouquet de Fleurs'.
'Seville'	■	■	■	■	■	■	Upright, thorny tree 20 to 30 feet high is used as a street tree in Arizona and Southern California. The seedy oranges make superior marmalade. Harvest time is the same as for 'Bouquet de Fleurs'.
MANDARIN (SEE PAGES 70–72)							
'Clementine' (Algerian tangerine)	■	■	■	■			Early variety with red-orange rind and juicy, sweet, variably seedy flesh. Fruit ripens fall into winter and holds very well on the tree. Light crop without a pollinator.
'Dancy'			■	■	■	■	Small, seedy, orange-red fruit is the traditional Christmas "tangerine." Needs high heat for a flavorful crop. Best crops are in Florida. Alternate bearer.
'Encore'		■	■	■			Very late variety with sweet-tart, seedy fruit that ripens from spring into summer and stores until fall. Alternate bearer.
'Fremont'		■	■		■		Early variety with seedy, richly sweet fruit. Alternate bearer.
'Honey'		■	■	■	■		Midseason California variety with seedy, very sweet fruit. Different from 'Murcott' tangor, which is marketed as Honey tangerine from Florida. Alternate bearer.
'Kara'	■	■					Springtime crop of sweet-tart fruit with varying seediness. Gets puffy soon after ripening. Best flavor inland; a little tart near the coast. Alternate bearer.
'Kinnow'	■	■	■				Midseason mandarin has seedy fruit too sweet for some people. Holds fairly well on the tree. Alternate bearer.
'Mediterranean' ('Willow Leaf')		■	■	■	■		Midseason crop of sweet, aromatic, very juicy fruit that gets puffy soon after maturity. Needs high heat. Alternate bearer.
'Pixie'	■	■		■			Late variety with seedless, mild, sweet fruit. Alternate bearer.
'Ponkan' (Chinese honey mandarin)	■	■		■		■	Early crop of seedy, very sweet fruit. Alternate bearer.
Satsuma	■			■	■		Very early mandarin with mild, sweet fruit. Succeeds in areas too cold for most citrus. Ripe fruit deteriorates quickly on the tree, but keeps well in cool storage. Selections include 'Owari', 'Dobashi Beni', 'Okitsu Wase', and 'Kimbrough'.
'Wilking'		■	■	■			Midseason variety with juicy, rich, distinctive flavor. Stores fairly well on the tree. Alternate bearer.
TANGELO (MANDARIN X GRAPEFRUIT; SEE PAGE 73)							
'Minneola'		■	■	■		■	Winter crop of bright orange-red, often necked fruit with a rich, tart flavor and some seeds. Best in hot climates and with a pollinator.
'Orlando'		■	■	■		■	Mild, sweet, fairly seedy fruit ripens about a month earlier than that of 'Minneola'. Best in hot climates and with a pollinator.
TANGOR (MANDARIN X SWEET ORANGE; SEE PAGE 73–74)							
'Murcott'		■		■		■	Very sweet, seedy, yellowish orange fruit ripens winter into spring. Fresh fruit is marketed as Honey tangerine. Alternate bearer.
'Ortanique'			■	■		■	Sweet, juicy, variably seedy fruit ripens in spring to summer.
'Temple'			■			■	Winter to spring crop of sweet to tart, seedy fruit. Needs high heat; fruit tastes too acidic in moderate climates. Tree is more cold-sensitive than other tangors.

■ Upper Gulf Coast = Gulf Coast from north of Corpus Christi, Texas, through Louisiana, Mississippi, and Alabama; Florida north and west of Gainesville
■ Florida = Central and southern Florida

	Cool Calif.	Mod. Calif.	Desert	So. Texas	Upper G. C.	Florida	
OTHER MANDARIN HYBRIDS (SEE PAGES 74–75)							
'Ambersweet'		■		■		■	Relatively new variety is the result of crossing a hybrid of 'Clementine' mandarin and 'Orlando' tangelo with a midseason orange. Juicy fruit borne in fall to winter is classified as an orange by fresh fruit marketers. Becomes very seedy when grown near another variety.
'Fairchild'		■	■	■			'Clementine' x 'Orlando' hybrid bears juicy, sweet fruit in winter. Best in desert. Produces a higher yield with a pollinator.
'Fallglo'		■	■			■	Fairly new hybrid that is somewhat cold-sensitive, like its 'Temple' parent. Juicy, tart, very seedy fruit ripens in fall.
'Lee'		■	■	■		■	Cross between 'Clementine' mandarin and an unknown pollen parent. Fairly seedy fruit matures in fall to winter. Best flavor in Florida.
'Nova'		■	■	■		■	'Clementine' mandarin x 'Orlando' tangelo hybrid. Juicy, richly sweet fruit ripens in fall to winter. Needs a pollinator.
'Osceola'						■	Not as good as 'Robinson', though developed at the same time and from the same parents. Ripens in fall. Needs a pollinator.
'Page'		■	■	■		■	'Clementine' mandarin x 'Minneola' tangelo hybrid. Profuse bearer, producing small, juicy, sweet fruit from fall into winter. Few seeds, even with a pollinator to improve fruit set.
'Robinson'		■				■	'Clementine' mandarin x 'Orlando' tangelo hybrid ripens its very sweet fruit in fall. Quite seedy with a pollinator. Best flavor in Florida.
'Sunburst'			■	■		■	Cross between 'Robinson' and 'Osceola' hybrids. Big, sweet, red-orange fruit ripens in late fall. Nearly seedless without a pollinator. Best flavor in Florida.
'Wekiwa' (Pink tangelo, 'Lavender Gem')		■	■	■		■	A tangelolo—looks like a small grapefruit, but its juicy, mild, sweet flesh is eaten like a mandarin. The flesh is purplish rose in hot climates. Ripens from late fall into winter. Not widely available.
SOUR-ACID MANDARIN (SEE PAGE 76)							
Calamondin	■	■	■	■	■	■	Mandarin-kumquat hybrid has fruit like a very small orange but with a sweet, edible rind. Juicy, tart flesh has some seeds. Plant is nearly everbearing in mild climates, and also fruits exceptionally well indoors. Variegated form is especially ornamental.
'Rangpur'	■	■	■	■	■	■	Acidic, seedy, orange-colored fruit is a lime substitute. Everbearing in mild regions; fruits well indoors. 'Otaheite' (Tahiti orange) is an acidless form sold as a houseplant.
PUMMELO (SEE PAGE 77)							
'Chandler'		■	■	■		■	Round-fruited, pink-fleshed California variety is the most commonly grown. Ripens winter to spring. Needs heat to develop color and sweetness. Good plant for espalier.
'Hirado Buntan'		■	■	■		■	The pink-fleshed pummelo with the sweetest flavor in Florida, where it ripens in early winter. The big fruit is round to slightly flattened. The large tree is a seedling of a white-fleshed Japanese variety.
'Reinking'		■	■	■		■	White-fleshed California variety ripens winter to spring. The pear-shaped fruit is bigger than that of 'Chandler' and not as sweet. The tree is also a little larger.
'Tahitian' ('Sarawak')		■	■	■		■	Small tree producing large, pear-shaped, white-fleshed, moderately acidic fruit with a lime undertone. Ripens winter to spring.
GRAPEFRUIT (SEE PAGES 78–79)							
'Duncan'		■	■	■		■	The oldest known grapefruit variety in Florida and the one from which all the others developed. Extremely seedy white flesh with better flavor than modern seedless types is great for juice.
'Flame'		■	■	■		■	Now being widely planted in Florida, this variety has red flesh similar to that of 'Rio Red', slight rind blush, and few to no seeds.
'Marsh' ('Marsh Seedless')		■	■	■		■	Lack of seeds made this seedling of 'Duncan' the main white-fleshed commercial variety. 'Pink Marsh' ('Thompson') is a pigmented form, but its color doesn't hold.
'Melogold'	■	■					Grapefruit-pummelo hybrid developed in California. Needs less heat than true grapefruit, though fruit doesn't hold as long on the tree. Seedless white flesh is sweeter than that of sister variety 'Oroblanco'; tree tolerates slightly more cold than 'Oroblanco'.
'Oroblanco'	■	■					Grapefruit-pummelo hybrid with same low-heat requirement as 'Melogold'. Fruit containing few to no seeds has a thicker rind and a more sweet-tart flavor than 'Melogold'.
'Ray Ruby' 'Henderson'		■	■	■		■	Almost identical seedless varieties have good rind blush and flesh pigmentation.

■ Cool California = Coastal and other cool-summer areas of California   ■ Moderate California = Warm inland and coastal valleys of California
■ Desert = Low desert of California and low and intermediate deserts of Arizona   ■ South Texas = Lower Rio Grande Valley north to Corpus Christi

	Cool Calif.	Mod. Calif.	Desert	So. Texas	Upper G. C.	Florida	
'Redblush' ('Ruby', 'Ruby Red')		■	■	■		■	Seedless grapefruit with red-tinted rind. Red internal color doesn't hold, fading to pink and then to buff by the end of the season.
'Rio Red'		■	■	■		■	Seedless variety with good rind blush and flesh nearly as red as that of 'Star Ruby'. It's a more dependable fruit producer than 'Star Ruby'.
'Star Ruby'		■		■		■	Seedless grapefruit with the reddest color, though the tree is prone to cold damage, erratic bearing, and other growing problems. Doesn't withstand desert heat.
LEMON (SEE PAGES 80–81)							
'Bearss'						■	Selection of a Sicilian variety grown in Florida; no relation to 'Bearss' lime. The fruit looks and tastes like that of 'Eureka'. Some fruit all year, but main crop in fall and winter.
'Eureka'	■	■	■	■		■	The familiar lemon sold in grocery stores. Some fruit borne all year in mild climates. Big, vigorous, nearly thornless plant to about 20 feet tall needs periodic pruning. Good for espalier.
'Improved Meyer'	■	■	■	■	■	■	Hybrid between a lemon and a sweet orange or mandarin; more cold-tolerant than a true lemon. Produces rounded, yellow-orange, juicy fruit with few seeds throughout the year. Naturally dwarf plant can grow 15 feet high but is usually smaller. This variety isn't permitted in Arizona.
'Lisbon'	■	■	■	■			The fruit is similar to that of 'Eureka' and is also sold in grocery stores, but the tree is bigger and thornier and can stand a bit more cold. 'Lisbon Seedless' is the same without seeds. These are the best lemons for the desert. Some fruit produced all year in mild climates.
'Ponderosa' (American Wonder)	■	■	■			■	Naturally dwarf, thorny lemon-citron hybrid. Throughout the year, produces seedy, thick-skinned, moderately juicy fruit weighing up to 2 pounds. Plant is more susceptible to cold than a true lemon. Thrives indoors.
'Variegated Pink' ('Pink Lemonade')	■	■	■	■		■	Sport of 'Eureka' with green-and-white leaves and green stripes on immature fruit. Light pink flesh doesn't need heat to develop color. Plant isn't as vigorous as 'Eureka', growing only about 8 feet high.
LIME (SEE PAGES 82–83)							
'Bearss' 'Persian' ('Tahiti')	■	■	■	■		■	The big-fruited, seedless lime sold in grocery stores. Called 'Bearss' in the West and 'Persian' or 'Tahiti' elsewhere. Some fruit all year. Needs less heat for fruiting and tolerates more cold than 'Mexican'.
'Kieffer'	■	■	■	■		■	Leaves are used in Thai and Cambodian cooking, as is bumpy, sour spring fruit. Available mainly in California.
'Mexican' ('Key', West Indian, bartender's lime)		■	■	■			Very thorny plant bearing small, rounded, intensely flavored fruit throughout the year. 'Mexican Thornless' is the same, minus the spines. Plants need high heat and are very cold-sensitive.
'Palestine Sweet'	■	■	■	■		■	Acidless lime that looks like 'Bearss' or 'Persian' and is used in Middle Eastern, Indian, and Latin American cooking. Fruit ripens fall or winter.
KUMQUAT (SEE PAGES 84–85)							
'Hong Kong' (Golden bean)	■	■	■	■	■	■	Very thorny ornamental variety with tiny, inedible fruit.
'Marumi'	■	■	■	■	■	■	Slightly thorny plant bears round fruit that is smaller than 'Meiwa'. Peel is sweeter than 'Nagami' but slightly seedy flesh is more acidic. Needs chilly nights during fall or winter ripening. Fruit can hang on for up to a year.
'Meiwa'	■	■	■	■	■	■	Round fruit is sweeter, juicier, and less seedy than that of other varieties. Also performs better than other types in cool-summer areas. Considered the best kumquat for eating fresh. Ripens and stores on the tree like 'Marumi'.
'Nagami'	■	■	■	■	■	■	Main commercial variety. Oval-shaped, slightly seedy fruit is more abundant and sweeter in hot-summer climates. Ripens and stores on the tree like 'Marumi'. Thornless plant is good for espalier.
LIMEQUAT (SEE PAGE 86)							
'Eustis'	■	■	■	■	■	■	Hybrid between 'Mexican' lime and round 'Marumi' kumquat is more cold-tolerant and needs less heat than its lime parent. Fruit shaped like a big olive has few seeds, sour juice, and edible peel. Some fruit all year, but main crop fall to spring.
'Tavares'	■	■	■	■	■	■	Hybrid between 'Mexican' lime and oval 'Nagami' kumquat takes more cold and needs less heat than its lime parent. Elongated oval fruit has same qualities and harvest time as 'Eustis'. A more compact, better-looking plant than 'Eustis'.

■ Upper Gulf Coast = Gulf Coast from north of Corpus Christi, Texas, through Louisiana, Mississippi, and Alabama; Florida north and west of Gainesville
■ Florida = Central and southern Florida

Cool Calif. ■
Mod. Calif. ■
Desert ■
So. Texas ■
Upper G. C. ■
Florida ■

ORANGEQUAT (SEE PAGE 86)

Variety	Cool Calif.	Mod. Calif.	Desert	So. Texas	Upper G. C.	Florida	Description
'Nippon'	■	■	■	■	■	■	Cold-tolerant hybrid between 'Meiwa' kumquat and satsuma mandarin has a fairly low heat requirement. Small, round, deep orange fruit with a sweet, spongy rind and slightly acidic flesh has a sweeter overall flavor than a kumquat when eaten whole. Fruit is borne in winter and spring, but holds for months.

CITRON (SEE PAGE 87)

Variety	Cool Calif.	Mod. Calif.	Desert	So. Texas	Upper G. C.	Florida	Description
'Buddha's Hand'	■	■	■			■	Homely plant bears big, fragrant fruit divided into "fingers" containing all rind and no pulp. Some fruit borne all year. Plant tolerates no frost. It might do as well as 'Etrog' in South Texas, but it isn't typically grown there.
'Etrog'	■	■	■	■		■	Straggly plant produces fragrant fruit like a big, warty-skinned lemon with dry pulp. Important in the Jewish Feast of the Tabernacles. Some fruit borne all year. Plant tolerates no frost, though in South Texas it often comes back after dying to the ground.

HARDY CITRUS (SEE PAGES 88–89)

Australian razzelquat	Shrubby plant bears sweet-tart, rather dry fruit with lemon-lime flavor. Ripens in summer. Good for arid or humid climates to about 14°F/–10°C.
'Changsha' mandarin	Similar to satsuma mandarin but not as flavorful. Ripens from fall into winter; dehydrates if not harvested promptly. Sometimes grown in Texas, Gulf Coast, and Southwest regions too cold for regular mandarin varieties. Hardy to about 5°F/–15°C.
Citrange	Hybrid between sweet orange and trifoliate orange. Old variety 'Morton' has fruit like a slightly tart sweet orange. 'US-119' is newer and sweeter. Fruit ripens in late fall. Hardy to between 10°F/–12°C and 5°F/–15°C.
Ichang papeda (Ichang lemon)	Fruit looks like a lemon but with big seeds. Ripens in early fall. Withstands subzero temperatures.
Khasi papeda	Fruit similar to a grapefruit but with a peppery tang. Ripens a few weeks after Ichang papeda. Hardiness listed at 15°F/–9°C but reported to withstand considerably more cold.
Nansho daidai	Big orange-colored fruit with seedy, sour flesh is eaten like a grapefruit or squeezed for juice. Ripens in fall. Hardy to at least 0°F/–18°C and withstands even lower temperatures with some protection.
'Thomasville' citrangequat	Developed from a trifoliate orange, kumquat, and sweet orange. Small, nearly seedless fruit is used as lime substitute if picked soon after ripening in fall. Left on the tree, it may become sweet enough to eat fresh. Hardy to about 0°F/–18°C.
Trifoliate orange	Extremely thorny deciduous shrub or small tree with fragrant flowers and inedible fruit makes an unusual specimen or barrier. Hardy to about –20°F/–29°C. 'Flying Dragon', a natural dwarf with curved thorns, survives to about –15°F/–26°C.
'Yuzu' ichandarin	Natural mandarin hybrid is a commercial variety in Japan. Big-seeded yellow fruit with mildly sweet, lemony flavor ripens fall into winter; it can be eaten fresh or used in cooking. Hardy to about 0°F/–18°C.

■ Cool California = Coastal and other cool-summer areas of California   ■ Moderate California = Warm inland and coastal valleys of California
■ Desert = Low desert of California and low and intermediate deserts of Arizona   ■ South Texas = Lower Rio Grande Valley north to Corpus Christi
■ Upper Gulf Coast = Gulf Coast from north of Corpus Christi, Texas, through Louisiana, Mississippi, and Alabama; Florida north and west of Gainesville
■ Florida = Central and southern Florida

INDEX

....

Photographers

The American Phytopathological Society: 52 right; 53-4; 55 middle, right; 57-1, 57-2, 57-3, 57-4; 58 middle; 59-4. **Scott Atkinson:** 24 top left; 25 top right. **Jerry Black:** 6. **Crandall & Crandall:** 13 top; 46 left, middle; 52 middle. **William B. Dewey:** 11; 23 bottom right; 62. **Gerald Frederick:** 28. **David Goldberg:** 2; 18; 24 bottom; 25 top left, bottom left; 50; back cover. **Saxon Holt:** 21. **Horticultural Photography:** 5 top; 15; 37 right. **Ells Marugg:** 24 top right. **Michael McConkey:** 9. **Robert J. McNeil:** 43; 53-1; 54 right; 56 middle; 58 right; 59-3. **Pam Peirce:** 8 top; 13 bottom; 14; 42. **Jim Rosen/Terraphotographics/ BPS:** 12. **Bill Ross:** 23 top right. **Teri Sandison:** 22 right. **SuperStock:** 4. **K. Bryan Swezey:** 40. **Michael S. Thompson:** 39. **Darrow Watt:** 46 right; 48; 90. **Ron West:** 55 left. **Guy Witney:** 37 left; 53-3, 53-5; 54 left; 56 left, right; 57-5, 57-6; 58 left. **Cynthia Woodyard:** 5 bottom. **Glenn Wright:** 59-2. **Tom Wyatt:** 8; 22 left; 25 bottom right. **Charles Youtsey/Florida Department of Agriculture, Division of Plant Industry:** 34. **Bob Zuckerman:** 52 left; 53-2; 59-1.